GOD'S

EMBRACING

LOVE

J.M.J.

God urges us to speak
tenderly to the hearts of
His people!

Our duty is to speak comfort
to God's people.

GOD'S EMBRACING LOVE

By

Reverend Father

Ralph Anthony DiOrio, Jr.

WITH ACKNOWLEDGMENT
TO THE SECRETARIAL STAFF

of

THE APOSTOLATE
OF
DIVINE MERCY AND HEALING

CHRISTINA PATTERSON
ALDONA SARKAUSKAS
DEBRA CARTER SEAMAN

Cover Oil Painting

By

Artist and Friend

Guy Danella

Utica, N.Y.

ISBN: 0-9754016-0-2

Library of Congress Control Number: 2004092553

Welcome
to the Ministry of
Divine Mercy
and
Healing

To Teach....
To Preach....
To Heal....

"The healing of man occasions nothing more but an event which creates faith."

PROPAGANDA FIDEI....
.... SANATIO HOMINIS

The proclaiming of The Faith....
.... The healing of Man

God's Healing Love

"You Are

My

People

And

I Love You"

A PRAYER FOR HEALING

Lord, You have told us to ask and we will receive,
  to seek and we will find,
  to knock and You will open the door to us.

I trust in Your love for me
  and in the healing power of Your compassion.
I praise You and thank You for the mercy You have shown to me.
Lord, I am sorry for all my sins.
I ask for Your help in renouncing the sinful patterns of my life.
I accept with all my heart Your forgiving love.

And I ask for the grace to be aware
  of the disorders that exist within myself.
Let me not offend You by my weak human nature
  or by my impatience, resentment or neglect
  of people who are a part of my life.
Rather, teach me the gift of understanding and
  the ability to forgive, just as You continue to forgive me.

I seek Your strength and Your peace so that I may become
  Your instrument in sharing those gifts with others.
Guide me in my prayer that I might know what needs to be healed
  and how to ask You for that healing.
It is You, Lord, Whom I seek.
Please enter the door of my heart
  and fill me with the presence of Your Spirit now and forever.
I thank You, Lord, for doing this.
                                        Amen.

MY

SPECIAL

DEDICATION

TO

BISHOP BERNARD J. FLANAGAN

And

MOTHER MOLLIE P. DiORIO

*Lord our God, You are the glory of
believers and the life of the just.*

*Open the arms of Your mercy
to Your faithful servant, Bernard.*

*As You created him in Your own image
and called him for Your service,
welcome him for ever into the
Presence of Christ in whom he trusted
and whose Gospel he preached.*

*We ask this through our Lord Jesus Christ,
Your Son, who lives and reigns with You
and the Holy Spirit,
one God, for ever and ever. Amen.*

Most Rev. Bernard J. Flanagan

**Born—March 31, 1908
Ordained a Priest—December 8, 1931
Consecrated First Bishop of Norwich—
November 30, 1953
Transferred to Worcester—August 12, 1959
Died—January 28, 1998**

RESPICE AD MARIAM

In Gratitude

To
the Memory
of

Bishop Bernard J. Flanagan, DD

**Spiritual Father and Mentor
to me
during the ministerial years of my
Diocesan Priesthood
and
The Healing Apostolate to the Sick**

MOLLIE ISMALIA PAZIENZA DiORIO
BORN~JULY 1, 1909
REPOSE IN THE LORD~JULY 17, 2003
INTERRED JULY 19, 2003

Memory Thoughts

- ❖ "Never Let Anyone Nor Anything Steal Your Peace."
- ❖ "Wake Up Smiling!"
- ❖ "Walk Straight! Head Up Always! Face the Storms: There's a Rainbow Above! Be a Victor in Apparent Defeat!"
- ❖ "Always Walk with a Good Conscience. God Strikes with a Cotton Hammer."
- ❖ "Be All Priest or No Priest at All!"
- ❖ "Be Good Children and ALWAYS walk as I taught you."
- ❖ "Keep in step even if others do not walk the straight line."
- ❖ "Be always yourself and yourself only!"
- ❖ "God Is Always God; and man will always remain man."
- ❖ "Priests are 'Alter Christus'—Other Christs! Don't condemn them. They have a mother who loves them."
- ❖ "Pray for Priests; Sacrifice for them."
- ❖ "Keep your vows holy. A vow confirms a promise."
- ❖ "The spirit of holiness in women is not lost, only forgotten. Let the world come to know that basically the problem of people is that they are in danger of losing holiness. Why? Only because they try to live on Broadways, on Avenues, on Streets of earthly misvalues. Thereupon, they end up in losing their spirit of sacrifice."

AND
EVERLASTING
LOVE

To the memory of my recently deceased mother,
Mollie Ismalia Pazienza DiOrio
Whose ninety-four years of unfailing loyalty,
devoted sacrifice, and unconditional love
Guided me
In my being God's priest and minister to all
mankind.

At her knees did I learn the truth of
Substantial love
For God, for all mankind, and for the respectful
dignity
Which affirmatively belongs
To the nobility of
Womanhood

J.M.J.

All proceeds from the sale of this book will be utilized for the non-profit ministries of the Father Ralph A. DiOrio, Jr. Foundation, Inc.

And

the National and International Ministry of The Apostolate of Divine Mercy and Healing

CONTENTS

THE GOSPEL MESSAGE OF HEALING

Fr. Ralph A. DiOrio—the Joy of Soulwinning

But you, be sober in all things, endure hardship, do the work of an evangelist, fulfill your ministry. (2 Timothy 4: 5)

SECTION
I

Introductory
Preamble

To Teach—To Preach—To Heal

J.M.J.

Help me, O Lord, to teach the beauty of Your ways so that yearning souls may find the Christ; and they too, in turn, will go out to witness Him to others.

J.M.J.

FROM THE DESK

OF

FATHER
RALPH ANTHONY
DiORIO, JR.

PREVIEW

REFLECTIVE INSIGHTS

FOR

THE SPIRITUAL JOURNEY

Holy Land—Along the Sea of Galilee

Every great ship asks for deep waters...
"Launch out into the deep and let down
your nets for a catch..."
When Peter made Christ the captain of his
boat he was commanded "To Launch Out"
into the deep! When Christ was in control,
Peter could no longer stay in the shallows.

JESUS SPEAKS

IN THE SPIRIT AND IN THE FRUIT

OF

HEALING LOVE

THROUGH THE HOLY SPIRIT

HOW?

IN

LOVE - JOY - PEACE

PATIENCE

KINDNESS - GOODNESS

FAITHFULNESS

GENTLENESS

SELF-CONTROL

MY
PRAYER
IS
TO BE PRESENT TO YOU

DEAR FATHER, AND ALMIGHTY GOD,
WHO DWELLS NOT ONLY
IN THE PORTALS OF HEAVEN,
BUT IN ALL YOUR CREATIONS,
IN ME, HEAR THIS PRAYER FROM THE
DEPTHS OF MY HEART.

FORM IN ME THE LIKENESS OF YOUR SON,
DEEPEN HIS LIFE WITHIN ME.
THEN I KNOW THAT I SHALL BE PLEASING
TO YOU, THAT I WILL BE
SUFFICIENTLY ADEQUATE IN
PRAISING YOU,
IN THANKING YOU,
IN BEING FORGIVEN IN YOUR HOLY LOVE.

I MAKE MY PRAYER OF SUPPLICATION
NOT ONLY FOR PETITION PRAYER FOR
MYSELF,
BUT HAVING CHRIST LIVING IN ME,
I SUPPLICATE MY PRAYER FOR
INTERCESSORY CONCERNS FOR ALL THIS
OUR MANKIND,
AND FOR THIS OUR BROKEN WOUNDED
WORLD.

SEND US, SEND ME, AS A WITNESS
OF GOSPEL JOY
INTO A WORLD OF FRAGILE PEACE
AND OF BROKEN PROMISES.
TOUCH THE HEARTS OF ALL MEN
WITH YOUR LOVE THAT THEY
IN TURN, AS A WORLD ALTAR CALL,
WILL RESPONSE IN LOVING YOU—
AND IN LOVING YOU, LOVE ONE ANOTHER.

    AMEN.

A PRAYER OF HOPE

FOR

YOU OUR READERS

**MAY THIS PRAYER, MAY THIS BOOK OF
VARIETY OF INSPIRATIONS
          BE PLEASING,
          BE HEALING,
          BE ENRICHINGLY AND
EVANGELISTICALLY FRUITFUL
TO ALL WHO WOULD DARE TO ENTER THIS
JOURNEY OF READING.**

**THE LORD BLESS YOU
          AND KEEP YOU;
THE LORD MAKE HIS FACE SHINE UPON
YOU AND BE GRACIOUS TO YOU; THE LORD
MAKE HIS FACE SHINE TOWARD YOU
AND GIVE YOU PEACE.**

MAY HOLY MARY, MOTHER OF GOD,
CHOSEN BY THE DIVINE PLAN,
GIFTED BY THE HOLY SPIRIT'S
      INDWELLING,
PRAY AND INTERCEDE FOR YOU.
MAY THE HOLY MOTHER PROTECT YOU
WITH HER MATERNAL CARE;
MAY SHE GUIDE YOU TO THE PORTALS OF
YOUR HEAVENLY ETERNAL DESTINY.

FATHER RALPH A. DiORIO

FROM THE DESK OF FATHER RALPH
A Special Message to My Readers

THE TRAGEDY OF LIFE IS WHAT DIES INSIDE A MAN WHILE HE LIVES

TO YOU, MY READING FRIENDS:
IT IS A TREMENDOUS JOY FOR ME TO INTRODUCE TO YOU A NEW BOOK AFTER HAVING WRITTEN MANY OTHERS SOME YEARS AGO. ONE NEVER GROWS OLD ENOUGH NOT TO SHARE A CUP OF BLESSING WITH ANOTHER.

REASON FOR WRITING THIS BOOK AND OTHERS TO COME:
THE MANY VOICES OF MY VAST AND WIDESPREAD HEALING MINISTRY, AS WELL AS THE MULTITUDINOUS AUDIENCES BOTH HERE WITHIN THE UNITED STATES AND ABROAD, WHERE FOR THE PAST TWENTY-SEVEN YEARS THE EVANGELIZATION AND HEALING MINISTRY BROUGHT ME, HAVE BEEN FREQUENTLY ASKING ME TO RECOMMENCE THE EVANGELISTIC TASK OF BOOK WRITING AND PUBLICATIONS. IT IS FOR THIS PRIMARY REASON, THEREFORE, THAT I ONCE AGAIN TAKE UP MY PEN FROM MY LIFE OF PRAYER AND MY

APOSTOLATE OF HEALING WORK TO
WRITE, TO PRODUCE AND TO PUBLISH
FURTHER WHOLESOME AND INVIGORATING
LITERATURE THROUGH BOOK MEDIA. WE,
THEREFORE, ARE JOYFULLY TO DO SO
WITH A RESPONSIBLE AND MOST
EFFICIENT COMPANY, THAT BEING, TAN
BOOKS & PUBLISHERS, INC. LOCATED IN
ROCKFORD, ILLINOIS.

MY FOCAL POINT IN WRITING:
MY AIM, WHICH NATURALLY FLOWS FROM
MY PERSONALITY AND GOD-GIVEN GRACE,
IS ONLY TO INSPIRE, TO ENCOURAGE, TO
MOTIVATE, AND TO EVANGELIZE SOME
"TRUTHFUL TRUTHS" THAT EXIST IN AND
FROM AN HONEST LOYAL GOD, NAMELY,
THE REALISTIC FACT THAT EACH AND
EVERY HUMAN BEING, WHATEVER THAT
LIFE HAS BECOME, IS INDEED PRECIOUS.
LIFE IS A GIFT. LIFE IS A PRECIOUS
SACRED GIFT. NOBODY SHOULD TAKE IT
FOR GRANTED. LET IT NOT BE
SQUANDERED. NOBODY SHOULD ABUSE IT
EITHER IN THEMSELVES NOR TO ANOTHER
WHO STANDS IN NEED OF SOME MEASURE
OF TRUTHFUL AFFIRMATION, AND
CERTAINLY THE NEED FOR LOVE.

MAY THE CONTENTS HEREIN WRITTEN BE A POWERFUL SOURCE OF ILLUMINATION, PURIFICATION, AND AN AFFIRMATIVE RESTORATION FROM THE SACRED HEART OF THE LORD. MAY IT EMPOWER EACH OF YOU WHO WALK THROUGH THESE PAGES AS A FRESHLY NEW ANOINTING IN HIS HOLY SPIRIT. LET IT BE FOR YOU AND FOR YOUR JOURNEY THROUGH LIFE "FIRM FOOT STEPS" TO THE CREATOR'S ETERNAL EMBRACE.

A REFLECTIVE THOUGHT:
As the rose in bloom cannot live without water, so are the memorable authentic and true stories of God's demonstrated care and love, narrated in descriptive simplicity, honest humility, heartfelt gratitude, and responsible accountability, the divine living waters of God's nourishment to peoples of all races and creeds. Oh, how enrichingly exciting it is to hear or to read real human and divine stories about real people in need of a God who is supposedly way up there, but who makes Himself known in the thoughts of Rocky Graziano the boxer: "Somebody up there likes me."

STORIES ARE FOREVER:

Everybody loves a story! Everybody loves a good story! Stories are powerful! Stories influence people! Good stories are always willing to be told again. Inspirational stories are always worth retelling. They come to us each day in a thousand and a million different ways. Some come as the spoken word; some touch our lives as written narratives, be they either fictional or real. Others capture our imagination; they in turn imprintingly brand and influence our thinking. Many stories cause us to react rather than act; or even, yes, to act upon them as we subjectively interpret them.

At times when we undergo different emotions, we ingest the stories we are exposed to, and we may apply their presented media themes as supposedly being the answers in resolving our daily encounters and problems. Some media data, unfortunately, may be misapplied to life, and thereupon cause many a person to pay an extremely enormous and heavy price causing severe personal, family, and social detriment—all because of unhealthy, irresponsible, and dangerous communication, be it personal subjective misinterpretation, or misapplication solutions to wounded life. What a disaster to the precious human person! It disintegrates a human spirit and soul; it leaves the catastrophic tragedy observed in so many lives, and that being the greatest tragedy of life about that which dies inside a man, a woman, a youngster, a teen, or a senior adult having grown old in the wisdom of life, mature in the hard years of attempting to be successful and able to fly in a hurricane.

STORIES HAVE MANY AVENUES:
STORIES ARE BORN FROM THE FIRST MOMENT MAN COULD COMMUNICATE WITH HIMSELF, WITH HIS CREATOR, WITH A FELLOW HUMAN CREATURE:

In this our day and age, in these our modern times, some stories come to us from those places we call our home, or from that family living room, or from the kitchen area where we comfortably and conveniently have placed our recorders, or our other technical media communication inputs such as the radio, the tape deck, or from that visual tube called television. There are so, so many avenues for story telling—so very many and impossible for pages to classify.

THE POWER OF A STORY:

Nevertheless, stories are forever! Why so? Because for many persons stories are powerful. Stories offer people a star and a rainbow of hope. They sensitively awaken the spirit of a sleeping giant within waiting to be born from the depths of a possibly frustrated, wounded human soul. Many a tear is shed; many a cry is wept; joys and pleasures burst forth in all forms, sizes and shapes; a host of other emotional tangents of the human heart, spirit and soul are stimulated—stimulated to good or even to bad.

Oh, the influential power of communication! May the media of storytelling in communication—those who use this God-given grace to share thoughts—be cognizant to their responsibility of consequences to other human beings; may they realize that such productions give birth to concepts, and such conceptual thoughts produce actions, good or evil. May communication honestly reflect upon its tremendous power to either make or break a precious human life, or even its power to destroy or to make a better world humanity. The power of the communication of stories is indeed veritably vast and influencing. But how essentially wonderful it is! What an amazing force to make the world a better place in which to live!

STORIES CAN ENRICH:
Did you ever realize that stories also have the energy to enrich and to invigorate human persons from rags to riches, from sinner to saint, and to many other lofty heights—heights never fathomed as possible?
Stories even have a tremendous psychological influence to make men out of little boys, women out of little girls, brokenness into strength, victors out of apparent defeat.

THIS BOOK:
In this book, another among many other wonderfully authored books of inspiration, you will journey into an experience of a very simple book presentation of communication. Its content is somewhat multiple in format. You will find separate individual parts, each in itself probably enough for a booklet all its own. They are, nevertheless, linked for and to a unified focal point. This focal point is to

inspire, to encourage, to motivate many a searching person to the love of the Almighty.

It invites the reader to experience the never-failing strength which through the sound and healthy communication medium of prayer accomplishes when it is directed to the distinctive person and agency of the divine healing mercy, the Holy Spirit.

For this reason, I have instructively added a section dealing with this Holy Agency of our Blessed Healing Savior who absolutely did not leave us abandoned when He returned to the Heavenly Father. He left us the Holy Spirit of His Father and Himself.
(St. John 16: 1-16)

WHY EMPHASIZE THIS ESSENTIAL DOCTRINE IN A POPULAR FORM?
The fourth section in this book enthusiastically presents itself as the essential doctrine about the Holy Spirit and the baptism in the Holy Spirit. I have presented it hopefully in a layman's easy popular grasp with reflective evangelistic meditations encircling it that you may comprehend them and accept them and

receive them in your unconditional surrendered spirit.... Why? Because I personally always believed that we who are trained in those theories "way up there," transmitted to us so as to primarily convince each of us that God is God, that whom and what we were studying and learned about would be of real veracity. In so believing, we, when the reality of multiple hurricanes in human living would arise—even against our vocations—none of us would abandon nor desecrate our committed promises to God and to God's people.

Come Back to Me With All Your Heart....
I Love You Still

YOU WHO ARE CHOSEN TO READ: YOU ARE CALLED....

Pray for us that we who are individually called by the Master to labor joyfully in His Holy Spirit may not leave in sacristies the so many beautiful empty chalices now abandoned by priests and ministers who for some reason fell short from being "victim servants." Pray for us; and pray for them to return to their calling. Please pray for so many of them whose shoes we have not walked in, but who left their first love. Scripture strongly states that people are being left behind without a shepherd—without the animating spoken divine word because pulpits of once gospel inspiration are now empty; altars once adorned for sacrificial reparation and divine restorative healing are left dirty and dusty.

WHAT STORIES, WHAT PRAYERS, WHAT MOTIVATING REFLECTIONS—AND WHAT CAN THE HOLY SPIRIT DO FOR YOU?

The data of this book unifies and links the various chapters into a pleasant and helpful source for fiery inspiration. They are beneficial thoughts which will lead to action—good healthy behavior.

Their power—especially the personally told narratives, the stories told and permitted for print by the people themselves—is hopefully geared in leading the reader to a personal evangelistic "altar call," to an "Adsum"—"Here I am, Lord, for You did call me."
(1 Samuel 3: 6)

"Behold I come to do Your will." (Hebrews 10: 9) The divine purpose in the use of this medium of book publication is definitely meant to have you fall in the arms of a God who never has forgotten you / us, even if the distractions of human living steal from each of us those precious, quiet, requiem, revealing moments between God and man and man with his God.

MY PRAYER, MY HOPE:
It is prayerfully trusted that the contents of this written presentation will help you, our reader, to know that even if life during those trying distinctive stormy moments does demonstrate itself in the poetical tones of the poet as being no rose without a thorn, no crown without a cross, there, nevertheless, does exist for both you and me, and for every human person on this side of heaven's door, the power that you can make it.

WHY READ?
Moments spent in reading can possibly become for a reader "the Magic of a

Miracle" as they can affirm a person in need and in search. Decent wholesome reading activates a communicative strength to comfort and to prompt another human "wounded sparrow" to rise and not be afraid to live again. It eventually leads them from a sense of gratitude to tell their true story, to testify as only they themselves can proclaim the everlasting divine love story. They can proclaim that others bogged down as once they were with human weakness can rise and be healed through the divine strength.

IS THERE ANYONE REALLY UP THERE TO HEAR MY CRY?

The book as a whole intends to disclose the method of authentic human cries. The data herein written reveals human hopes in their searching for something valuable, for someone "really real," for somebody with whom living human beings can comfortably talk, present their concerns, confide their apparent desperate longings without being rejected. In life we never hurt another by loving them; we only hurt another by rejecting them. Then, after all things are done, everything heard and tried, the reader will come to the joyful relaxation that communication with the author and creator of life, God Himself, is worth the journey of trust.

PEOPLE JUST NEED TO SPEAK:
People who know "what time of the day it is," or as the New Yorkers would amusingly say "are not out to lunch," are People who speak to People through the art of communication. People just simply need to communicate with reliable persons, with persons upon whom they can place their trust. One of the worst pains is to have another break trust. This disloyalty is also the painful anguish of divorce that another broke trust.

People with faith have trust. People of faith and hope speak to their God. People who speak to God meet the Almighty in His full deity. These souls encounter the living three Persons of the Holy Trinity.

People speak to holy persons; people in their needs speak to their trusting saints. People daily speak to friends, relatives, even to strangers who may eventually

become friends. **People just need to speak!**
In such conversations, even with the Lord,
such folk honestly and trustingly do narrate
how faith and faith alone gives birth to
hope. In such conversation, talk or
communication, people come to finally
realize the reality of a rainbow beyond the
stars, a light beyond the darkened forest, a
journey of a discovery to the Divine
Invisible Power whose name is God. These
souls, really human beings with body, soul,
and spirit, are persons who have blood in
their veins, passions in their emotions.
They, after experiencing in a personal way
the Presence of God in anointing blessings,
gratefully and confidently stand tall.
Unafraid, but with holy boldness, just as the
Apostles did after the Pentecost experience
in the Holy Spirit, they proclaim The Living
God.

                                    (Acts 2; Acts 4)

HOW DO PEOPLE FIND GOD IN MOMENTS OF EXISTING NEED?

God uses people to help people. Bodies,
emotions, spirits need the healing of
wholeness. People through their brokenness
are providentially led to God's

visible demonstration of His helping Presence through the use of the Holy Spirit's selection and use of His chosen human channels. These human vessels of election and gifts serve as God's Postmen to teach, to preach, to heal, and to build afresh the broken Mystical Body of Our Lord. People are needed by God to go into the arena of the world.

God in every age sends His Presence: Through human men and women who are themselves in union with God, and who are willing to be God's extension of compassion, service, and visible charisms, God wills to send. In so sending to direct others to come the Holy Spirit demonstrates through these human agents of committed service, that the Church with the message to salvation is of paramount importance. With these signs and through the charismatic gifts there is the continuation in time of the various phases of God's Son, our Blessed Lord and Savior Jesus.

> *"I am with you until the end of time."*
> (St. John 14; 15; 16; 17)

How impressively beautiful are the thoughts of our Lord in these His last moments with His agents of choice, His apostles. In this beautiful Priestly prayer, He states that He will be with us until the end. Love never fails to find a way to stay in communication. May each of us, you and I, never forget. Read these chapters and find what love truly is all about.

Allow no hardships, no frustrations to control you to the point of abandoning His promise to be with us. Allow yourself never to desperately climb to the cliff of despair due to the onslaughts of human forces causing depression promoted by unresolved anger. He has not left you an orphan. That is why the Holy Spirit is necessary for daily existence.

DOES GOD REALLY HEAR? IF SO, DOES GOD RESPOND?

God not only hears, but He listens. He always responds to simple, honest and truthful communication with Him. This is called prayer. The prayer I speak about is clear, clean, honest thinking. It is speaking from the heart and from within the soul of a person who is convinced about the valid belief that there does exist a God, and that this God is the Almighty One of all the universe. God does respond! His response offers a love presence to whatever cause is leading us to humbly speak with Him, thus uniting us with Him both in time and in eternity.

MY PRAYERS COMPOSED JUST FOR YOU:

For this above reason, I have attached another section to this book and to these stories. It is a section with selected personal prayers composed by me in private times of prayer or at services of healing. Some are added to the main stories as told by the recipients of healing. Wherever you read throughout this book, just remember that these prayers are helps, and only helps for you. They are for anyone who may be overwhelmed with the duties and the vicissitudes of daily struggle.

A PRAYER—ALWAYS IN SPRINGTIME

A prayer which is a soul in union with God is a launching path for one who prays. Through examination and critique of oneself, prayer guides one to refocus. Some people who are experiencing the mixture of human cries and laughters become subjected to the changing episodes of the moment; but honest clear thinking prayer will redirect one on the road to restoration and to clarity of human life's purpose.

All things, therefore, so considered, such selected prayers remain only as launching paths to prayer with the Master and the Holy Spirit. They are just simple stepping-stones to launch a person into opening up the greatest and most precious area of their lives, their inner consciences, their very private and personal secrets to a God who loves them just as they are. Why not try it? You are in for a great expectation!

EVERYONE WHO SPEAKS WANTS DESPERATELY TO BE HEARD:

When one speaks, one wants to be heard. In every communication, everybody wants to be heard, especially when they cry. Everybody has a secret to eventually disclose. Everybody has a story to tell. Everybody wants a miracle. Who is it who does not in human terminology cry for "The Magic of A Miracle?"

Maybe you might just find it right here in this book which by God's Divine Providence wants to speak, to communicate a very special message to you.

Bless you, each and every one of you.

I remember you.   (Jeremiah 2: 2)

SINCERELY YOURS,

Father Ralph ✝

Father Ralph Anthony DiOrio, Jr.

Weekend Retreat—Waltham, Mass.
Healing the Broken Heart

SECTION
II

A Priest
and
His Call

And we shall be questioned
only about love!

About

FATHER RALPH ANTHONY DiORIO

PRIEST OF GOD

HEALING SERVANT

TO

GOD'S   WOUNDED HUMANITY

" SERVIRE, REGNARE EST "

TO SERVE IS TO REIGN

Forever Thine

Vowed to Thy love, Thy livery I wear;

Into Thy hands my future I resign;

Grant, then, I beg, this earnest, whispered prayer;

Lord, keep my loving heart forever Thine.

Paths may be steep; life's skies may not be fair!

Whether the sun be darkened or it shines—

Calvary or Tabor's height, make this my prayer;

Lord, keep my loving heart forever Thine.

All through life's journey, Master, let me share

Thy Lordship's ways, Thy works let them be mine.

But in exchange, dear Lord, grant me this one

Prayer; Lord, keep my heart forever Thine.

The Priest and His Call

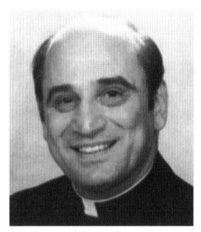

Father Ralph Anthony DiOrio

July 19, 1930	—	Born: Providence, Rhode Island
August 18, 1930	—	Baptized
September 8, 1945	—	Entered Seminary
September 8, 1949	—	Novitiate
October 7, 1950	—	Profession of Vows
June 1953	—	Bachelor of Arts and Letters
June 1, 1957	—	Ordained Priest
March 29, 1968	—	Diocese of Worcester Entrance
March 19, 1972	—	Incardinated as Diocesan Priest
June 1972	—	Post Graduate Degrees of Education
1972 - 1977	—	Spanish Apostolate Work
February 20, 1976	—	Charismatic Acceptance Ministry
May 9, 1976	—	Blessed with Charism of Healing
November 15, 1977	—	Founder of the Apostolate of Healing Worcester, MA
October 7, 1978	—	Appointed Director for the Apostolate of Prayer for Healing/Evangelism Office of Administration, Leicester, MA

1976 - *Years of Service to the Lord*

ILLINOIS
Chicago
Peoria
IOWA
Des Moines
Dubuque
Waterloo
KANSAS
Dodge City
Kansas City
Topeka
KENTUCKY
Covington
LOUISIANA
Lake Charles
Lafayette

ARKANSAS
Little Rock
CALIFORNIA
Orange
Sacramento
Stockton
CONNECTICUT
Bridgeport
COLORADO
Pueblo
DELAWARE
Wilmington

FLORIDA
Miami
Orlando
Pensacola-Tallahassee
St. Augustine
St. Petersburg
GEORGIA
Atlanta
HAWAII
Honolulu
IDAHO
Boise

MASSACHUSETTS
Boston
Springfield
Worcester
MICHIGAN
Detroit
Lansing
Grand Rapids
MINNESOTA
St. Cloud
St. Paul-Minneapolis
Duluth

**United States....Canada....Alaska....Mexico
West Indies....England....Ireland....India
The Holy Land....Philippines
Hawaii: Molokai Leper Colony**

**Europe:
Germany....Italy....Sicily....Spain....Poland
Portugal....France....Yugoslavia....**

Archdiocesan and Diocesan Crusades - **2004**

MISSOURI
Kansas City
St. Louis
MONTANA
Great Falls
Billings
Helena
NEBRASKA
Grand Island
Omaha
NEVADA
Las Vegas
NEW HAMPSHIRE
Manchester
NEW JERSEY
Newark
Camden
NEW MEXICO
Albuquerque
NEW YORK
Albany
Brooklyn
Buffalo
New York City
Syracuse
Ogdensburg

NORTH CAROLINA
Charlotte
NORTH DAKOTA
Fargo
OHIO
Cleveland
Steubenville
Youngstown
OKLAHOMA
Oklahoma City
OREGON
Baker
PENNSYLVANIA
Allentown
Harrisburg
Scranton
SOUTH CAROLINA
Charleston
SOUTH DAKOTA
Sioux Falls
TEXAS
Amarillo
Brownsville
Corpus Christi
El Paso
Galveston-Houston
Laredo
Lubbock

San Antonio
Victoria
VERMONT
Bellows Falls
VIRGINIA
Arlington
Richmond
WASHINGTON
Spokane
WISCONSIN
Milwaukee
LaCrosse
CANADA
Ottawa
INDIA
Alleppey, Kerala
MEXICO
Laredo
WEST INDIES
Castries, Saint Lucia –
assigned services in
preparation of the Pope's
visit
ISRAEL, Jerusalem,
Galilee
ITALY, Rome
FRANCE, Lourdes

**Crusades
throughout
all of Italy
in three
summers...**

**From Milano
down into Sicily**

The Healing Spirit

To heal, not to injure
To help, not to hurt
To strengthen and sustain
With patience, compassion
and trust.

To unite, not to divide
To counsel, not to condemn
To reason and reconcile
Through peace, understanding
and love.

MAN of PRAYER
PRIEST of SERVICE

About Father Ralph A. DiOrio

Father DiOrio is a Roman Catholic Priest, Educator, Philanthropist, Author, Artist and Healer. Fr. DiOrio was ordained June 1, 1957, and has served in parishes in Chicago, IL; Ontario, Canada; Utica, NY; and Fitchburg, MA.

He is the recipient of the following awards:
Children's Village 1982 Angel Award,
UNICO's Man Of The Year Award – 1982,
Bishop O'Reilly Assembly Citizen Of The Year Award – 1997.

He has attained the following degrees:
-BA degree in Philosophy and Liberal Arts – St. Charles' Seminary, Staten Island, NY, in conjunction with St. Joseph's Archdiocesan Seminary, Dunwoodie, NY.
-Theology Studies and Priesthood – Sacred Heart Major Seminary, Melrose Park, IL, in conjunction with Mundeline Archdiocesan Major Seminary, Mundeline, IL.
-Masters Degree in Education (School Psychology Major) – Fitchburg State College, Fitchburg, MA; BFA – Degree in Fine Arts, Cum Laude, University of Massachusetts, Amherst, MA.

Doctor of Humane Letters – Anna Maria College, Paxton, MA; Certified by the Commonwealth of Massachusetts – In Latin, Spanish and Italian. He also holds certificates as a School Psychologist and a Counseling Psychologist.

Fr. DiOrio's concern for world humanity resulted in creation of his Children's Fund. The Fund's accomplishments include a Children's Hospital – Alleppey, India, and a Children's Clinic addition and a Chapel for the Benedictine Sisters – St. Lucia (West Indies).

Fr. DiOrio received the Gift of Healing on May 9, 1976. On November 15, 1977, his International Healing Ministry was formed, taking him all over the world. Many people have witnessed healings at the crusades. In India, a crowd of 250,000 people attended one such service. He has been written about in countless newspapers and magazines, and has had the privilege of appearing on National and International TV and Radio. Fr. DiOrio has a well-established

Audio and Video ministry, **and is the** author of eight books. Additional publications are in the process of production through TAN Publishers, Rockford, IL.

Under the faithful adherence to the sound theology of the Church, and under the obedient and prudent supervision of the local bishops of Worcester, past and present, and under the overseeing general authorization of the Holy See's officials, Father Ralph Anthony DiOrio, Jr. is permitted to function in these services of evangelization and healing – as long as he preaches and teaches the mercy and the love of Jesus Christ.

The teaching and preaching brings about the expression of faith and the occasion of healing. God chooses many ways to convey His love, namely the teaching and preaching of the Gospel. It has been discerned by appropriate authority that Father DiOrio, during the past 26 years of the formal healing ministry throughout the world, fulfills his responsible accountability to Almighty God and to the People of God.

In the spirit of this anointed priest, we of the Apostolate of Divine Mercy and Healing, extend the soul and spirit of Father Ralph – as he is publicly and affectionately called – the blessings which have been participated and extended throughout the world:

"May the blessings of Almighty God, the Father, the Son, and the Holy Spirit descend upon you; and may the protection of the Holy Mother of God, Mary most blessed, be upon you and protect you on your earthly voyage from here into eternity. Amen."

MY PRAYER

Father Ralph's Special Prayer
for
Our Reading Audience

Dear Blessed Lord,
In the name of the people, both here and far away, I take this opportunity to pray to You. We are certain that You are our Lord, that You are our Savior, You are our Divine Healer.

In my own person I now profoundly and personally thank You for Your everlasting Presence among us, but in me especially, since I am uttering this prayer. How immensely grateful I personally am for the countless gifts You continue to gift me!

With all my soul I thank You for the gift of life, the gift of family, the grace of having sincere friends. These are truly precious priceless gifts. Help me never, never to abuse them. Forgive me if in some past moments throughout the span of my life I have willingly acted in a spirit of recklessness, even in carelessness. If I did so, Lord, then I know now that I have offended You, You who dwell in them, and You in me. Thank You, Lord, for this opportunity of personal insight to my spirit and to my soul. Thank You!

Lord, today as I have invested in the purchase of this simple book by Father Ralph and his staff, I cannot help but think that it is another one of Your ways to invite me to be exactly what You created me for. You never give up on me, do You? Thank You for Your patience.

Dear Lord, are You at this moment gently laughing at me? This my present spiritual experience does sound amusing, doesn't it, as through them I come to my senses in the evaluation of the realistic priorities of human existence. You know, it does take time to crash into this my hard-shelled self-centered idolatry! But, Lord, I am happy for this quiet moment of truth with You, and You with me. My heart, through the purpose and influence of this book, is meeting You in this gracious rendezvous of love, of divine healing restoration!

Lord Jesus, this world of materialism is so distractive; its glamour appears thrilling for only a "tickling moment." In the last analysis, however, how truly vain–empty it is.

Nevertheless, I must confess that at times, I, in fact, so many, many foolish times, did become engulfed with this world's many facets of excitement. Victimized by them, I have written many stupid chapters in my autobiography; but in the long run, even in those moments of frustrated need searchings, I came to realize that the frivolous "world trinkets" and its fleeting cravings are not permanent. They make a promise which they cannot permanently keep. In fact, they do not make me really happy; they are only impassioned stimulating toys to make me momentarily comfortable. Sometimes they end up as "tinny sounds," corny broken instruments, as promises which are not kept by their first attractive invitation.

Dear Lord, as I am undergoing at this moment this "knocking" of You at the door of my spirit, may I ask if You really are listening to my heart? This conversation with You is extremely important to me in what I am wanting to say. Lord, please listen! Please do not just hear "words without thoughts which do not ascend into heaven." This special thought which I want You to receive is very important for me to have You listen and to accept. It is this:

If by chance, anyone or anything in my life has taken me away from You, or if I have given my love elsewhere to frail inconsistent creatures over You, then help me, because only You can do this rectification, only You can make everything all freshly new.

As I read this simple book of inspiration and motivation that "I can make it," then I am absolutely certain that this moment in this day is Your day. This day of reading is an opportunity to think cleanly and clearly into what real prayer is all about. When this is so, then the open door of heaven's miracles shower abundant graces upon me and upon the Divine Guidance hovering my earthly intended assignments.

Yes! Thank You, Lord, for listening to me. Thank You, Lord, for granting me the grace to obtain another inspiring opportunity through this medium of book inspiration, to become a "Victor" in my daily apparent "Storms." In your abundant heart of love, dear Lord, give me strength renewed to search Your paths, to hear Your voice, to read Your word, and to let burn within my heart Your sacred fire of divine love.

Lord, all the favors I have received come through Your generosity. Do not let them return to You empty.

LET THEM BEAR FRUIT!

Healer of body and spirit, comfort the sick.
Be my Healing Physician today.
Be present today to the dying.
In Your mercy, visit and refresh me.
Renew all of wounded humanity.

Dear Mother Mary, Mother chosen by God Himself for your maternal assignment, be our Mother! Pray for us.

My Prayer:

Lord, I want at this very second in this my life span to receive You as my personal Lord and Savior. Both You and I know that I, like all humans from that first moment of pride and disobedience in that garden once created holy, inherited the wounds, the consequences, and brokenness of original sin.

Dear Precious Jesus, I believe that You died for me out of pure love for me. I believe that death had no hold over You, and that You triumphed over death when You rose from the dead on the third day. I confess that I am a sinner. I need Your love and Your forgiveness. Come now into my life as You have never come before. Forgive me my sins, and give me eternal life. I proclaim You right now as my Lord and my Saving God. Thank You for Your peace, Your joy, Your healing love.

Only You can restore and heal.   Amen.

Fr. Ralph A. DiOrio

"My Greatest Love Has Always Been The Missions Of The Church"

To save a soul is the most precious opportunity in the life of a man or woman called by God to one's fellow man.

"God has found us worthy to be ministers of His Gospel, and so we boldly speak—we strive to please God and not men."
(1 Thessalonians 2: 3-4)

What God has given us is good for the world!

In God's Divine Providence, we are going to take it to the world!

The World is God's parish, and He has unfolded that World parish through the trustful hands of human persons who have a heart of devotion, a soul of honesty, and a spirit of total consumption.

Pray daily that the World of you and me may touch the five continents of this universe with the five precious bleeding wounds of the Lord and Savior, Jesus Christ. The World is yours if you just touch it!

LAUNCH OUT INTO THE DEEP

God always confirms His message with signs and wonders—miracles!

People all over the world—masses of people—are waiting for the Church to return to her knees in fasting and prayer, asking God as the early Church did: "Grant unto Your servants that with all boldness they may speak Your word, by stretching forth Your hands to heal; and that signs and wonders may be done by the name of Your holy Child Jesus."
(Acts 4: 29-30)

THE GOSPEL AND HEALING LOVE

The message of the Gospel comes from our dear Lord and Savior Jesus Himself.

In very simple visible form, the Gospel and Healing Love **is Jesus dwelling and working in and through His praying and laboring followers—men, women, teens, children, seniors. Goal:** Operation **Gospel Divine Blessing and Healing Love!**

The Lord fills His people with the empowering gift of the Holy Spirit. Miracles become born! Signs and wonders of sorts burst forth in bodies, in souls, and above all, in the spirit.

What do people cry for? What do people look for? What really do people long and pray for?

God gives people the desires of their hearts.

**"Call to Me in times of trouble.
I will save you, and you will honor Me."**

Psalm 50:15

ALL HEARTS WHO TURN TO TRUSTFUL HUMAN AGENTS ARE REALLY SEEKING A SAVIOR WHO SPEAKS THE LANGUAGE OF LOVE, HONESTY, TRUTH, TRUST, AND WHO TENDERLY CARES FOR HIS OWN.

TWO BROTHERS MEET!

They have the same Mother:
    The Church.

They have the same Father:
    God the Father.

They have the same Brother:
    Christ our Lord.

They have the same Spirit:
    The Holy Spirit.

They eat the same Bread:
    The Eucharist.

They drink from the same Cup:
    The Chalice.

They love the same Woman:
    Our Lady.

They work in the same City:
    The City of God.

Prayer, Evangelization, and Healing Crusade, St. Lucia, Castries, West Indies—In Preparatory Services for the Papal visit of Pope John Paul II, as directed by Rev. Father Ralph A. DiOrio, diocesan priest of Worcester, Massachusetts, U.S.A.

"THANK YOU,

THANK YOU,

THANK YOU FOR SERVING THE CHURCH.

I BLESS YOU AND THE APOSTOLATE OF HEALING.
IN YOUR MISSION TO THE CHURCH, NEVER, NEVER COMPROMISE THE GOSPEL OF OUR LORD JESUS CHRIST."

God's Embracing Love

Little Child Healed of Deafness

Photograph taken at St. Lucia Crusade (Two-Week Crusade of Preaching, Teaching and Healing among the people of St. Lucia, West Indies)

Services were conducted as a preparation for the Archdiocese population for the oncoming visit of Pope John Paul II,
July 1987

To TEACH—TO PREACH—TO HEAL—IS A NOBLE TASK! ~Lyndon B. Johnson

ONLY BELIEVE:

They who had scorned the thought of any strength except their own to lean on, learned at length how fear can sabotage the bravest heart. But human weakness answering to the prod of terror calls, "Help us, O God!" And silence lets the silent voice be heard, bringing its message like a spoken word:

"BELIEVE!
BELIEVE IN ME!
CAST OUT YOUR FEAR.
OH, I'M NOT UP THERE
BEYOND THE SKY,
BUT HERE,
RIGHT HERE IN YOUR HEART.
I AM THE STRENGTH YOU SEEK.
BELIEVE!
ONLY BELIEVE!"
And they believed!
(God Is My Co-Pilot)

(Reprint with permission of the Worcester Telegram & Gazette)

Touched by the Lord—Healed in the Spirit
The Joy of Healing

Kristin Petrasek, daughter of Mark & Theresa

**And her children shall rise up—run to her and bless her,
and thank her for the gift of life.**

SECTION III

Motivational
Reflection

The greatest love story in all the world is God's love for you. There are thousands of people who have burdens to be lifted, problems to be solved, and Sin that needs to be forgiven. Thousands stand at the crossroads of decision. But Divine strength is not usually given until we are fully aware of our weaknesses.

YOU CAN BE A WINNER

NOT A LOSER

What a privilege to speak comfort to God's people....

"Give Comfort, Give Comfort to My People."

To all of God's Children:
"There is no difference between the Jew and the
Greek: for the same Lord over all is rich unto all that
call upon Him." (Romans 10: 12)

*Lord, lead me to someone who needs a friend. May
I not be too busy to recognize Your leading.*

CONTENTS OUTLINE

<u>YOU CAN BE A WINNER NOT A LOSER</u>

IF YOU HAVE

MET CHRIST,

GO FORTH

AND PROCLAIM

HIM TO THE

WORLD!

POPE JOHN PAUL II

BEING A WINNER AND NOT A LOSER

PART ONE

Would you like to be a winner?
Would you like never to be a loser?
Would you like to win the jackpot?

Would you like to be healthy again?
Would you like to live again?
Would you like to have a new chance?
Would you like to write a new chapter in the
    autobiography of your life?
Would you like to live for a purpose?

You can be a winner, not a loser.
You can win the best of life.
You can be restored to health again.
You can live your assignment—your purpose
for being.

REFLECTION

**IT IS SUCH A JOY TO SEE PEOPLE
SUCCEED WITH THEIR LIVES:**
**It is such a tremendous joy to be with you
through the written word. Maybe someday
we will meet. Maybe someday I will have
my priestly joy of blessing you in the name
of the Divine Healer.**

**God is a very good God. He loves what He
created just like a devoted and true parent
who loves, sacrifices, and even would die
for his or her child.**

**God gives beautiful blessings. So, even
through the written word such as a book,
God sends a message of love all packaged
up in different blessings. Even a book can
be God's message sender—God's Postman!**

ONLY A TOUCH AWAY:
**Something beautiful is in store for you as
you accept His love package. Just reach
out in whatever way you can, and only
believe! Just eagerly seize it. YOUR
BLESSING IS ONLY A PRAYER AND A
TOUCH AWAY!**
It is in your heart.

God's touch of love and healing all comes in the package of a love story. This package or this bucket full of blessings is God loving you and you recognizing that love, and you unconditionally responding to that love relationship.
It has to be All or Nothing at All!

Points to launch out into the depths of being a winner:

A-   As the artist treasures his skillful completed painting, and as the master craftsman prides in the quality of his labors, so it is with the Master Creator in you.

B-   Do you love dreams?
      Many beautiful things are found in
         dreams.
      God gives us dreams—good dreams!
      God gives us goals—achievements to
         fulfill.
      We have a purpose for living.
      God gives us excellence for life.
      God gifts us with charisms.
      God makes each of us special.
      God offers us our right to happiness that we may enjoy His life shared in us.

C- Do you feel you are a loser?
Do you feel just about defeated?
What has happened to you to steal the
best in you?

(Galatians 1:6)

D- Let me tell you something real, very
real, and something exceptionally
powerful. It already dwells in you. God
put it there when He permitted life to
enter you. You can be a winner! You
don't have to be a loser! You don't
have to be defeated. This victory is a
miracle power, and it is closer to you
than you think. The miracle is not way
out there. It is not in someone earthly;
not in something material and
eventually decaying. It is not in empty
promises which the world tries to
offer, but seldom keeps its promises.
Where is this miracle? The miracle is
in the house. The "magic of miracle"
is in your heart.

E- You know where the answer is, don't
you? As you enter your heart, your
thoughts, your conscience, as you
peacefully reflect in the Presence of
God who loves you just as you are, you
become honest with your truthful
convictions. The magic of your miracle
is not in power. Such fades away. It is
not in money. Money only makes us

comfortable; it does not give us happiness.

F-   The answer is in Him and in Him alone; it is in our God who made us. He knows every part of us. That Person is the Heavenly Creator's visible extension of Himself. That visible Person is our Blessed Lord, Jesus.

G-   Jesus is God.
Jesus is our Savior.
Jesus is our Healing Physician.
Jesus is our life.
There is nobody like Jesus.

H-   Problems exist.
Everybody has problems.

I-   Jesus is a problem solver.

J-   Successful people, it is said, are problem solvers.

K-   All types of people can become successful problem solvers. These are the winners; these are the victors! Lawyers are successful if they solve

legal problems; doctors are successful if they solve physical problems; Priests, Rabbis, and Ministers are successful when they influence souls; computer experts are successful if they adjust our laymen's limited knowledge of this powerful modern writer; husbands and wives are successful if they know how to love without limits.

You have problems. Welcome to this world. You can be a fixer. You can be a warrior.

You can be a victor in human apparent defeat.

CONSIDERATIONS

1- **SO MANY PEOPLE CAME TO JESUS:**
They came with their problems. They confidently brought their own sicknesses, their various diseases. They brought their little children that Jesus would tenderly and compassionately touch, hold, and bless them.

Jesus was where they were, where they needed help. Jesus loved them dearly.
Many do not even know there is a God who made them, who loves them in spite of their failings. How sad this ignorant catastrophe is!

2- **THOUSANDS CAME TO OUR BLESSED LORD.**
They came burdened with:
  their guilt,
  their sin,
  their sicknesses.
  Some came with just their love.

3- **JESUS OFFERED A NEW CHANCE:**
When one walks in, through, and with the Lord Jesus, one will always find clean new chapters to write anew for one's journey in life. Jesus offers opportunities to start all over again. Who does not want a new chance? Everybody likes to hear or read stories of new beginnings, new opportunities, a passage to victory.

Jesus offers every human being the graces to renewal. These are:
  CLEANLINESS—FORGIVENESS—FRIENDSHIP—A
    BETTER TOMORROW—ETERNAL LIFE

BUT WHAT IS THE MOST TERRIBLE OF ALL AILMENTS?

THOUSANDS CAME WITH SPIRITUALLY STARVED SOULS AND SPIRITS. HUNGER IS A TERRIBLE POVERTY. IT CAUSES UNTOLD AND UNCLASSIFIED— AT TIMES SERIOUS—VIOLENCE. BUT THE HUNGER OF THE SOUL IS WORSE.

4-   The Lord Jesus has an answer. His answer was His very own self. Jesus said: "I am the Bread of Life etc." (John 6: 35)

5-   Hundreds who approached Him did so with bodies riddled with sicknesses and diseases, with evil spirits, hurts of all sorts; but the most tragic of all the wounds were and are those of the dejected and the broken spirit, the wounded soul in its depressed emotions. And the worst of all, is that sin and its consequences. Sin never pays off in the end.

All case stories who have willingly accepted sin as a way to life have all come to cry the tears of further devastation, sorrow, and remorse. Some who could not find someone to lead them to the rivers of living water gave up through suicide, drugs, other escapisms which eventually showed them that irrational living behavior did not pay off. What a drastic situation exists when one indulges and lives ignorantly and foolishly. Psychologists and theologians in their ascetical and moral findings identify such behavior as insanity.

APPLICATION TO BEING A WINNER, NOT A LOSER

PART TWO

CONFIDENCE needs to be lifted up.

Obstacles might exist:
You may have a problem way down deep inside of you. You may be afraid to share it for fear of self-exposure or the possibility of being rejected. This is the greatest wound of wounds and of suffering—to be rejected, not loved. You may not be able to trust someone with your very personal problem: v.g.:
... your son with a problem.
... your daughter may be having a divorce.
... a husband who is sick, or alcoholic.
... a wife that left you for another love.
... a husband who fell into adultery.
... you may be left abandoned with no income.
... you may have children with no father.
... you may have children to raise, and no income.
... you are overwhelmed with bills to pay and you don't know what to do.

DON'T LOSE FAITH!

There is a Road that leads to a Ray of Light. **TURN TO THE LORD.** Cast all things unto the Lord.

PROBLEMS CAN BE A VISION TO REALITY: They break our self-indulgence and our pride. They remove arrogance from us. **THEY MAKE US DEPENDENT ON GOD FIRST. DON'T LOSE SIGHT OF WHAT GOD HAS IN STORE FOR YOU. SURRENDER YOUR PAIN. PAIN IS REALLY DEEP. REAL PAIN IS DEEP AND VERY PERSONAL.**

HOW CAN YOU HELP YOURSELF?

The answer is **WITH GOD'S GRACE** working affirmatively in, with, and through you.

BE A WINNER EVEN WHEN EVERYTHING SEEMS USELESS.

Are you at the crossroads in your life? How do you conquer? You have the "stuff" in you that makes for a warrior, a winner, and not a loser!

WELCOME TO THE WORLD

PART THREE

WE ARE HUMANS:
Don't try to run away from this inevitable fact!

You are human with all its contents! You have a body; you have a soul; you have a spirit. You live in a world. In this world there are many things; but most of all, in this world there are other humans. In this world you relate to them; these and they relate to you. Something sensitive occurs.

The question at hand is how do you affect the world around you, and how does the world around you affect you? Only you can answer this relationship be it for better or for worse. In spite of the response, there is always a rainbow of hope for a person who comes to know who they are, who their Creator is, and then the answer becomes so easy in the fact that we come to know the catechism's first chapter question: the reason and the purpose of our creation.

Today at this very moment of your reading, you are being invited to an incredible moment of deliberation which must lead to a moment of decision. God through His Son, Jesus, and through the agency of the Holy Spirit, gives you this opportunity. It is just for you! It is all yours. Nobody can have the power to take it away from you, except you yourself in a refusal to stand tall and to live again. If you step out in faith, and just trustfully surrender to Him, you will be surprised that all this pleasantry of inspiration and words can objectively make a difference. You know what? It will help you be a winner, not a loser.

TAKE HOLD OF THIS CHANCE

PART FOUR

Momma used to say that there are no chances, nor circumstances in life. There are only blessings.

So, maybe rather than use the mundane word of "chance"—as wonderfully as this word refers to various concepts—maybe we can just rename it as "BLESSINGS" (FROM HEAVEN).

GOD ALWAYS HAS A BLESSING FOR YOU:

It is yours!

Your miracle is in it!

Somewhere, somehow, there exists a blessing just for you! That is why God uses a thousand and one and more avenues to speak to you, and to eventually through His invitation to you, receive your unconditional surrender to His love and to His plan for you. So, look up and don't look down! Don't miss your blessings!

YOU SAY THAT YOU ARE HURTING:
Everybody hurts somewhere, somehow.
Everybody needs healing in some area.
Wounds are many:

> **emotions**
> **minds**
> **memories**
> **body afflictions**
> **circumstances**

THERE'S A MIRACLE FOR YOU. THERE'S A HEALER OF BROKEN DREAMS. THERE'S A DIVINE PHYSICIAN FOR WOUNDED LIVES. THERE'S A GOD WHO WALKS WITH YOU ALONG THE STREETS OF SORROW, ALONG THE BOULEVARDS OF BROKEN DREAMS. IT IS THE DIVINE TROUBADOUR OF LOVE. IT IS OUR LORD AND SAVIOR. THE MIRACLE IS IN JESUS. THE MIRACLE IS FOR YOU! YOU ARE GOD'S MIRACLE VESSEL. YOU ARE A VESSEL OF ELECTION!

WHAT TO DO?
CHANGE THE CHANNEL IN YOUR LIFE'S TELEVISION PROGRAM. TUNE IN TO THE STATION!
Get rid of or redirect (?) i.e. (you know what or whom!) Use your memory about the great things God has done in you and for you. Rejoice in what He will do for and with you. The big but small world of today needs you!

Nothing in the world can hurt you unless you allow it.

Read along with me the story of the barracuda and the Spanish mackerel. There was a glass between them. The barracuda kept trying to catch the mackerel, but the mirror in between prohibited it. The barracuda kept dashing against the glass and finally gave up. Later, the mirror was removed and the two fish swam together. The psychologist removed the mirror for this test. He proved victory can be won and evil will fail. Evils are blocks to the best in you.

The mirror was the symbol of the black, negative attitudes which make us losers.

God is the Mender of our lives.

Be like the eagle. It was meant to fly.

There is another story that you might relate to. It is the description of the baby eagle lost and found by chickens. It was raised by the chickens. One day the little eagle saw other eagles flying. He wanted to fly. The other chickens said to it that it was only a chicken, not an eagle, and that it could not fly. But the little eagle kept trying. And what do you know—it flew. You see, it had to be what it was made for.

You are made for higher things. You for God.

PRAYER:
Father, come to me now with Thy Holy Spirit. Help me in this my special need. Help me in turn to help another with their problem. Give me Your eyes to find those who need me. Thank You for creating me.

IF YOU ACCEPT JESUS WHAT HAPPENS?

PART FIVE

Every gift that is given is representative of the person giving the gift. No matter what the gift may be, all that matters is that the gift is a symbol of the person giving that expression of love.

When Jesus gives you a gift, you receive a gift from the Giver of all gifts. His gifts are best. Jesus gives the biggest gift of all: He gives Himself with the Father and the Holy Spirit.

Jesus in His gift-giving presents as a groom to a bride the opening chapter into a new life. It promises strength by imparting it in you. What are these precious gifts? They are:

> inner peace
> forgiveness
> healing and health
> prosperity and success
> assistance and solutions with
>   financial situations
> prosperity in all areas of human life

**WHY IS THIS GENEROSITY SO IMMENSE?
BECAUSE YOU ARE IMPORTANT TO HIM.
YOU ARE NOT AN ACCIDENT.
GOD PLANNED YOUR BIRTH FROM ALL
ETERNITY.
(JEREMIAH 1: 5)**

**GOD CAN SOLVE EVERY PROBLEM YOU
ARE IN.**

**HE DOES IT THROUGH A LOVE
RELATIONSHIP:**

HE TO YOU; YOU TO HIM.

It takes two to make real love, a love that is
truly worth everything to live for: God and
the human person He created out of love.

GOD WANTS YOU WELL

PART SIX

Along with God's gift, there is gifted health for the God-given span of your life. If you belong to God, then you will be nourished, cared for by incredible ways. Above all, God will sustain you with strength beyond human analysis. This is "gifts" to you and to me so that we will accomplish our earthly assignment as outlined in His purposeful creation of us. In descriptive language, it is simply so that you also can help light a candle for someone else who is in the darkness of their human journey.

WHAT IS YOUR ASSIGNMENT?
WHATEVER EXPERIENCES WE UNDERGO, THEY MUST OF NECESSITY LEAD TO THE SOCIAL GOSPEL. THIS IS NOTHING MORE THAN THE LORD'S COMMANDMENT TO LOVE ONE ANOTHER AS HE LOVES US.

**IT IS YOUR SEED FAITH:
IT COMES FROM GOD TO YOU AND FROM
YOU TO ANOTHER.
GOD HAS CREATED YOU FOR A PURPOSE, A
REASON TO LIVE.
V.G. MY MOTHER IN 1939, SERIOUSLY
SICK, WAS BROUGHT TO THE RHODE
ISLAND HOSPITAL. SHE PRAYED: "GOD
SAVE ME IF THIS LITTLE BOY NEEDS ME."**

**WHEN I WAS IN THEOLOGY AND VERY
SERIOUSLY ILL, I WAS BROUGHT TO OAK
PARK HOSPITAL IN OAK PARK, ILLINOIS,
AND SURGERY PERFORMED BY A
WONDERFUL GENTLE SURGEON, DR.
RIVERS, FOR AN ILLNESS AS
THEORETICALLY DIAGNOSED PRIOR TO
THE SURGERY, SUPPOSEDLY WITH CANCER
AND MEDICALLY STATED THAT I HAD ONLY
FOUR MONTHS TO LIVE, I MADE A SIMILAR
PRAYER.**

**IT WAS: "DEAR LORD JESUS, IF I AM TO
BECOME A BAD PRIEST, LORD, LET ME DIE;
IF NOT, LET ME LIVE FOR YOU AND FOR
THE WORLD."**

STORIES FOR EXAMPLE:
LIFE IS PRECIOUS:

1- THERE WAS A CRICKET IN THE HOUSE. I DID NOT HAVE THE HEART TO KILL IT. SO I FOUND A WAY TO FREE IT, AND THUS SAVED IT.

2- WHILE CUTTING THE GRASS AT MY PROPERTY RESIDENCE, I CAME UPON A SICK RABBIT. I PREPARED SOME FOOD FOR HIM, EVEN SOME ICE CREAM COVERED WITH SOME ITALIAN BRANDY. THE LITTLE RABBIT CONSUMED IT ALL. THEN OFF IT WENT. SOME MONTHS LATER IN SEPTEMBER, THE RABBIT—NOW GROWN SOMEWHAT—RETURNED, AND FRIENDLY AND UNAFRAID CAME AND SAT NEXT TO ME AS I WAS SITTING OUTSIDE WHILE TRYING TO SAY MY EVENING PRAYER OF VESPERS. ISN'T IT MARVELOUS HOW A LITTLE LOVE EVENTUALLY RETURNS TO THE SOURCE OF THE BLESSINGS!

3- THERE WAS ONE DAY A DARK BROWN/ BLACKISH BUTTERFLY IN MY PRIVATE PRAYER CHAPEL. IT WAS AT THE WINDOW TRAPPED BETWEEN THE SCREEN AND THE GLASS. I CAREFULLY, CAUTIOUSLY, AND SKILLFULLY MANAGED TO OPEN THE WINDOW FOR ITS ESCAPE. IT WORKED, AND THE BUTTERFLY FLEW AWAY FREE AND CONTENT. WE ALL HAVE POWER OVER LIFE, DON'T WE?

4- IN THE REAR OF MY RESIDENCE, ONE DAY I SAW AN UGLY SITUATION. THERE WAS A FROG CAUGHT BY AND IN THE MOUTH OF A SNAKE. I FREED THE FROG— SAVED IT—FROM THE MOUTH OF THE UGLY SNAKE. I KILLED THAT AWFUL SNEAKY SNAKE WITH MY RED RIDER BB GUN. EVIL MUST BE KILLED. SO TOO, SICKNESS— WHICH IS AN EVIL DEPRIVING US OF HEALTH, BROUGHT ABOUT BY ORIGINAL SIN AND ITS CONSEQUENCES—MUST BE KILLED. IT MUST BE ERADICATED FROM MAN!

CHRIST HIMSELF WAS ANGRY, VERY ANGRY AS HE WITNESSED SIN STEALING THE LIFE SO PRECIOUS TO GOD AND GIFTED TO MANKIND. BUT GOD DID SOMETHING POWERFUL ABOUT IT WHEN HE SENT HIMSELF IN THE PERSON OF HIS DIVINE SON, THE CHRIST. JESUS THE CHRIST IS THE ONLY DELIVERER AND HEALER. HE ALONE HAS THE POWER TO DO SO.

GOD MAKES LIFE BEAUTIFUL

PART SEVEN

HERE ARE SOME INCLUDED GUIDELINES TO HELP YOU ON YOUR VICTORIOUS JOURNEY.

MAN SPOILED LIFE BY THE DECEPTION OF THE EVIL ONE. JESUS REDEEMS LIFE AND RENEWS IT IN THE HOLY SPIRIT. THE HOLY SPIRIT SANCTIFIES LIFE, PRESERVES IT, SUSTAINS IT.

HOW IS YOUR LIFE ??? A DOCTOR CANNOT HEAL UNLESS THE PATIENT HONESTLY REVEALS TRUTHFULLY THE PAIN OF DISRUPTION—POSSIBLY DESTRUCTION AND DEATH.

PROTECT YOUR LIFE FROM ALL EVIL. BE JEALOUS OF YOUR SOUL.

RECOGNIZE THE MANY CAMOUFLAGED HINDRANCES TO VICTORY AND IN BECOMING THE WINNER:

1-   WATCH WHAT ENTERS YOU!

BE CAREFUL WHO COMES INTO YOUR HOUSE. NOT EVERY KNOCK ON THE DOOR IS A FRIEND.

2-   CONTROL UNNECESSARY CONFLICT.

IT IS A DISTURBANCE—A WASTE OF TIME. THERE'S A RIGHT TIME AND THERE'S AN UNWISE TIME TO APPROACH A PROBLEM, A SITUATION (ECCLES. 3— THIS CHAPTER IS A PROTOCOL OF RULES TO EDUCATE PROTEGEES ON THE JOURNEY. THEY ARE NOT JUST FAVORABLE TIPS).

3-   DON'T WASTE TIME WRITING TO A CRITIC OR EVEN TO A TRULY EVIL ONE. DISCERN AND ONLY DO WHAT IS NECESSARY, AND DO IT CONCLUSIVELY.

REMEMBER THAT WHAT YOU WRITE WITH A PEN, YOU CAN'T STRIKE OUT WITH AN AX.

4- WHEN YOU MUST CORRECT, DO IT APPROPRIATELY.

AS MY COUSIN LOUIS RAGOSTA TAUGHT ME—THAT IS: "SAY WHAT YOU MEAN; MEAN WHAT YOU SAY; AND DON'T BE MEAN WHEN YOU SAY IT."

5- YOU SHOULD BE SELECTIVE WHEN ATTACHING YOURSELF TO A MENTOR.

A MENTOR—HE OR SHE—RISKS FOR YOU. YOUR MENTOR SEES YOUR ENEMIES BEFORE YOU DO. OTHERS SEE WHAT WE DO NOT SEE.

6- SEEK TO DISCERN A PURE HEART IN ALL YOUR RELATIONSHIPS.

7- STAY FOCUSED ON GOD.

8- DISLOYALTY IS A REJECTION. IT USUALLY ENDS UP IN AN ANGER NURTURING UNHEALTHY BITTERNESS IN ALL PARTIES INVOLVED—ESPECIALLY IN THE ONE WHO DISLIKES YOU OR HATES YOU OR IS ENVIOUS OF YOU.

WHEN GOD WANTS TO BLESS YOU, HE LETS WRONG PEOPLE LEAVE YOU.

9-   AVOID THE CORRUPTION OF INNER BITTERNESS.

IF IT RESIDES IN YOU IT WILL EAT YOU. IT WILL CONSUME YOU.

10-   EVERY PERSON WHO MEETS YOU CARRIES AWAY A PIECE OF YOU— GOOD OR BAD!

11-   DON'T LOSE PEOPLE IF POSSIBLE. TRY TO LOOK UP TOGETHER.

SEE A RAINBOW OF HOPE. LOOK UP FOR THE SILVER LINING. IN BAD TIMES THE CAT AND THE DOG DRINK OUT OF THE SAME BOWL.

12-   THE LOVE OF JESUS IS OUR UNITY. REMAIN IN HIS LOVE.

A SOUL IN UNION WITH GOD IS ALWAYS IN SPRINGTIME. WE GO AS FAR AS OUR PRAYER.

13-   ALWAYS RESIST WHAT IS WRONG.

SIMPLY RESIST AND LET THE SPIRIT OF GOD TAKE OVER AND DEAL WITH YOUR ENEMIES. PLACE YOURSELF UNDER THE PRECIOUS SHED BLOOD OF CHRIST.

14- MANY OF YOUR DECISIONS DETERMINE YOUR FUTURE.

JUST AS YOU PUT MONEY ASIDE FOR YOUR FUTURE, DECIDE YOUR TACTICS IN A SPIRIT OF FAITH FOR VICTORIOUS LIVING. LET THE DIVINE GUIDANCE BE YOUR CONSCIENCE.

15- LOOK INTO THE INTERIOR OF A PERSON.

NOBODY IS TRULY SEEN AS THEY ARE FROM THEIR EXTERIOR. LOOK INTO THEIR EYES, AND YOU WILL INEVITABLY SEE THE SPIRIT WITHIN. NOT ALL PERSONS ARE SINCERE. LOOK BENEATH THE COSMETICS. SEE WITH A THIRD EYE; HEAR WITH A THIRD EAR.

16- LOVE GOD ABOVE EVERYONE AND EVERYTHING ELSE.

BE JEALOUS OF YOUR SOUL!

BLESSING YOU IN THE ABUNDANCE OF HIS GRACE, AND IN THE WISDOM OF THE HOLY SPIRIT~

GOD LOVE YOU,

FATHER RALPH

**There is only one force
the Church of God needs,
and that is**

The Spirit of God

SECTION IV

Power
In
The Spirit

Rev. Father Ralph A. DiOrio ~ Ordained June 1, 1957

A Priest Forever—Anointed In The Holy Spirit

"The Lord hath sworn, and He will not repent: Thou art a priest for ever according to the order of Melchisedech."

ANOINTED
IN
THE
HOLY SPIRIT

"A Priest Forever"

ADVENTURE

In

THE SPIRIT

A Journey of Life

In

The

Holy Spirit Baptism

I Am With You Still

OUTLINE CONTENTS
TO

THE BAPTISM IN THE SPIRIT

ADVENTURE IN THE SPIRIT

A Reading from the Acts of the Apostles
Acts 8: 14 - 17

In those days, when the apostles in Jerusalem heard that Samaria had accepted God's message, they sent Peter and John who went down to the Samaritans and prayed that they might receive the Holy Spirit. For it had not yet fallen on any of them; they had only been baptized in the name of the Lord Jesus. Then the two laid hands on them and they received the Holy Spirit.

Prayer

Dear Father in heaven, all hearts are open to You and every wish and secret is known. Cleanse our thoughts by the inpouring of the Holy Spirit and grant us the grace to love You perfectly and praise You worthily through Jesus Your Son. Amen.

J.M.J.

My Dear Friends and Readers;

1- THESE REFLECTIONS ARE BEING PRESENTED IN SOMEWHAT OF AN OUTLINE FORM.

2- WRITTEN AS SUCH, THEY CAN BE OF IMMEDIATE REFERENCE AS THEY SERVE YOU WITH SIMPLE CLARITY OF UNDERSTANDING.

3- THEY CONSIST MAINLY OF THE BASIC SUBSTANCE PERTAINING TO THIS POWERFUL AND VIVACIOUS DOCTRINE.

4- I HOPE THESE REFLECTIONS WILL BE HELPFUL TO YOU, MY READER. MAY GOD'S CARE AND CONCERN FOR YOU GENTLY MOTIVATE YOUR CONSCIENCE AND YOUR AWARENESS OF THIS NECESSARY LIFE FOR YOUR JOURNEY FROM HERE TO YOUR ETERNAL LIFE.

5- MAY THE HOLY TRINITY DRAW YOUR WHOLE BEING TO FALL IN LOVE WITH THE THIRD PERSON OF THE HOLY TRINITY. YES, FALL IN LOVE WITH HIM! Your life will never be the same!

6- YOUR LIFE IS ABOUT TO CHANGE
WHEN YOU WELCOME THE HOLY
SPIRIT INTO YOUR PERSONAL LIFE'S
JOURNEY. THE HOLY SPIRIT WILL
ACCOMPANY YOU ALONG THIS LIFE'S
JOURNEY OF YOUR DAILY REVELATION
—THE DISCOVERY OF YOUR PERSONAL
WORTH! YOU WILL SEE, WHOEVER YOU ARE,
THAT YOU ARE ONE OF GOD'S GREATEST
CREATIONS. HE WILL REVEAL IN HIS
DIVINE GUIDANCE YOUR PURPOSEFUL
JOURNEY OF REVELATION TO THAT
GLORIOUS CITY OF GOD WHERE THE
ALMIGHTY FATHER, SON, AND HOLY
SPIRIT—THESE THREE DIVINE PERSONS IN
ONE GOD WILL WELCOME YOU NOT AS A
STRANGER.

PART ONE

DOES SCRIPTURE HAVE SOMETHING TO SAY?

In the Old Testament, in the book of Wisdom 1: 7, which is considered by some as apocrypha (nice books, hidden books, not inspired, and therefore listed as not canonical), we read that the Spirit of the Lord fills the world, is all-embracing, and knows man's utterance.

We also read in Psalm 103: 30, "Send forth Your Spirit, and they shall be created; and You shall renew the face of the earth."

In the Church's scriptural history book written by St. Luke the Apostle, we read that suddenly there came a sound from heaven, as of a violent wind blowing, where they were sitting, and they were all filled with the Holy Spirit, speaking of the wonderful works of God.

You are about to read, and hopefully accept the Person of the Holy Spirit in a distinctive way, electrifying that which you received in water baptism by which you were made a Christian. May these pages be blessed by the Presence of the Lord, and may Almighty God grant your constant prayers that they may make you deserving of the Holy Spirit in a powerful burst of heavenly power that you may serve God's people in truth and justice, holiness and charisma. In so doing, you will be building up the Body of the Lord, and hopefully make one His Mystical Body, the Church. May the Lord forgive us our sins and transgressions that we will be worthy receptacles, worthy temples of that holy Presence.

Baptism IS VERY IMPORTANT TO SALVATION:

In the Ministry of Jesus:
It is stated in the Holy Scripture that our Blessed Lord submitted His human nature to this precious experience.

FOR YOUR PERSONAL READING AND PERSONAL INPUT THE FOLLOWING SCRIPTURES WILL BENEFIT YOU.

SUCH READING AND MEDITATION OVER THEM WILL MOTIVATE YOUR JOURNEY INTO GOD'S ANOINTING POWER, BOTH FOR YOU AND FOR OTHERS WHOM YOU ARE CALLED BY GOD AND HIS PURPOSE FOR YOUR BIRTH ON EARTH TO SHARE YOUR LIFE IN AND TO THE SOCIAL GOSPEL.

Scriptures:
JOYFUL AND EXCITING TO READ AND REFLECT:

Take a few moments right now and read your New Testament:

Mt. 3: 13 - 17

Mk. 1: 9-11
WHAT IS GOD SAYING TO YOU?

Luke 3: 21-22
AS YOU ARE READING THESE?

John 1: 20-3

Jesus and the Baptism:

Question of Importance:
Did our Blessed Lord consider and respect the grace of Baptism, and the baptism preached and performed by St. John the Baptist?

Jesus came to this earth to bear upon His shoulders the wisdom of the Crib which would lead to the strength of the Cross. This means that He was granted human exposure united to His Divine Person. This was the Christmas story of Who came to earth. BUT Why? Because He had to bear the burdens of His ministry. HE DID THIS

THROUGH HIS PREACHING, TEACHING, HEALING, AND BY HIS DEATH AND RESURRECTION (THIS IS THE "WHY" HE CAME TO THIS EARTH).

Why THE UGLINESS OF THE CROSS?
BECAUSE HE WAS BORN TO GO TO THE CROSS. IT WAS NOT REALLY PILATE WHO SENT JESUS TO THE CROSS; IT REALLY WAS HIS HEAVENLY FATHER WHO LOVED US SO MUCH THAT HE HIMSELF SENT HIS ONLY BELOVED SON FOR YOU AND FOR ME. OH, HOW SO VERY MUCH HE LOVED US.

In so doing, His sacrifice would be His conquest over Satan. He would be victorious over death which sin caused and by which it attached its sorrowful curse into the human life.

YOU, I, AND ALL THE WORLD WOULD HAVE A NEW CHANCE in the autobiography of our lives to redeemingly live again a life that is worth living. Because of our Lord, we would live in a living faith. Our journey would definitely be assured from here to eternity. Salvation would be ours. God keeps His promises.

Jesus For The Sake Of The Bystanders submitted His human nature to this distinct experience.

One could say that in His human nature He needed an empowering by the Holy Spirit which was performed by His cousin, St. John the Baptist.

The Heavenly Father broke the mysterious silence of that baptismal moment with the scriptural affirmation:

"This is My beloved Son, in whom I am well pleased." (cf. St. Matthew 3: 13-17)

Jesus permitted this baptism before He moved out into the arena of the world. His assignment was to preach the kingdom of the Father, to show The Father's Love and kindness, to offer salvation. Broken humanity could have a new chapter in their life's human history. It was nothing more than God's Love Story made visible.

God would not leave us, His human creatures, orphans. Our Heavenly Father would find a way to bring us safely home to His pleasing embrace, even if we who are of necessity under the penalty of original sin.

His everlasting love would never allow this terrible sin-tragedy, with its immediate transmission of so much unhappiness and catastrophic mental and physical pain as caused by the failure of Adam and his wife Eve, to deprive us the experience blessing of The Prodigal Child who safely came home to the reconciled peace of salvation.

As God, of course, He was not subject to such a baptism; but as the god-man, He willingly took on the nature of a servant:

He limited His humanity:
By way of example, He was born of a wonderful mother; her name was Mary, virgin and spouse of the Holy Spirit.

As her human son, He learned at her knee, grew up in submission. Like us, He received an anointing of the Holy Spirit before He took on the burdens and the brokenness of the world. He powerfully pronounced the kingdom at hand. Essentially He preached and taught that the love of the Father had not left us abandoned. Confirming His Godly Presence, He compassionately performed the healings of the sick. He powerfully performed deliverances from unkind and evil spirits, possessions, obsessions. He overpowered all sorts of evil. Amazing the crowds, but with love and compassion for the afflicted, He raised the dead.

All this He willingly and lovingly did. He who is great became small in the infinity of His earthly littleness.

He limited Himself in some way to be like us except for sin.

He had a plan for us—for us, His followers:

In order to keep His mission of salvation alive until the end of this earthly world, He would send His Holy Spirit into us—for every period of time. He would anoint us with the powers of the Holy Spirit, retaining and keeping alive for us and through us His followers the living phases of His own person. These would be the "Charisma of the Holy Spirit." (cf. 1 Corinthians 12; Eph. 4: 12)

Thus, we can do the same works as our Lord, i.e. exactly what Jesus did from His Baptism moment to the moment of the Cross. Pentecost would confirm that in us.

Because of God's eternal love and care for us, the Church was born. And so the miracle of the Crib, which would lead to the strength of the Cross, would be the substance for the heavenly Magic of Pentecost.

Magic seems to defy the ordinary with its apparent unexplainable feats, deeds of unusual daring and skills.

God, however, not a magician of fake, fraud, or counterfeit, does perform the greatest story ever told—that being, the eternal love story of a Creator whose love always finds a way for a prodigal child to peacefully return safely home. And you by His invitation are born with and for a cause. You are called to serve. You are called to love. You have a purpose. God equips you for service with His gifts!

PART TWO

BAPTISM IN THE SPIRIT

"Rivers of Living Water"
When we accept to be baptized in the Holy Spirit, we become like rivers of living water.

A soul in union with God is always in springtime. We stay holy by staying in union with God through the Holy Spirit. If we reject and adulterate our service as ministers, we thus are not fit to serve as ministers. God forgives us, yes, but we have forfeited our right to serve. We, therefore, if we are to serve effectively, need a life of repentance, a life of earnest prayer which keeps us in God's living Presence and in God's perspective. So let us always first try to become holy so that we, from a life of union with God, can be clean, clear, trustful instruments of grace to others.

Our prayer life, our virtues, etc. flow charismatically powerful because God's grace was there for us to accept and to live a daily union in His Presence.

Being Perfect Believers:

"Nemo dat quod non habet." Thus goes the old Roman adage. This means that we do not give what we do not possess. If we have God within us, then when we go to perform the Lord's intended assignment, we go and we do so because we are prepared to enter the arena of a world gone out of perspective.

The arena of this materialistic world has many a misconception and many a misapplication of the gifts of earthly goods. There are the dangers of adulterated philosophies, misconstrued morality rights, and a host of many other destructive forces. These forces are recognized in their spirit to split individuals and to split and break asunder community, eventually to separate the God-given human souls from their eternal salvation. How sad this is?

Without wholesome Godly-revealed dogma, there is no Godly goodness; without holy reasonable ethics and morality, without a solid and complete academic education in sound philosophy and theology, not a perfunctory exposure to piece-meal education, there is no true holistic perception to rock-solid happiness within the self, and then from the inner self to the neighbor—the social gospel, and ultimately unto God.

In such a status, mankind is dangerously playing a fatal game:

mankind is playing with fire.

PART THREE

BAPTISM IN THE SPIRIT

We Need Preparation:
A doctor, a teacher, a clergyman, or any other professional approved servant, is never blamed for his or her studying. We as human recipients request our public and religious officials to be abreast in those professional areas which serve to benefit us. It is a "condition without which" for proper appropriate service. It is a "conditio sine qua non."

Baptism Is In The Spirit:

Acts 1: 5
"John baptized in water, but within a few days you will be baptized with the Spirit."

BAPTISM IN THE SPIRIT:
What essentially is it? What is this exceptional bombastic experience which charismatic people so marvelously express, and from whence they have derived such an enriching relationship with God and with the Social Gospel? It is a tremendous joy to witness these happy and joyful souls. As with many other servants of the Lord

working in multiple areas of religious assignments, much positive credit and respect must be acknowledged to these people who are cognizant that members in all the churches are apparently stagnant. They appear expressively burnt out with their human efforts, their programs and their overworked "modus operandi," and their overplayed tunes of "ad hoc committees," as necessary as they may be. Such moments are naturally present. They are found in and at all times of history. Everybody, not only in church affairs, but in every vocation or labor of life struggles to survive, and has fallen victim of various boredoms.

Perhaps an answer is found in and through the promises of Christ Jesus. Perhaps, as we see others successful and victorious in the front line of various battles, what is needed is a fresh anointing by God Himself in what activates new life. We see it in the promise of the Holy Spirit. We have witnessed it in the past, and we see it continuing in our day. It is without question, a New Pentecost. Such an experience sanctifies our human talents, anoints our persons. It imparts and elevates the God-given gifts of charisma through the fire of the Holy Spirit. It is grace working upon, elevating our human nature as St. Paul, so theologically correct, describes. It is in church terminology "GRATIA SUPPLET NATURAM."

So many times it is seen that man strains himself in labors of doing good, but eventually cries out for some absolute strengthening force of help. But on earth there is nothing absolute. This struggle is something as that of the apostles. It is so very reminiscent of the hard-working apostles in their fishing boat where they anguishingly attempted on their own efforts to wade the storm of the sea. It strained them by their useless human efforts. In such a fearful segment of their lives, so frightening in the powers of the awesome natural forces of nature, the angry, voluminous, engulfing sea, they suddenly remembered the Presence of the Lord Jesus, who, pretendingly or not, was sleeping in the rear of that little fisherman's craft. He awaited their cry for help. We all at some time in our lives cry, really cry desperately for help just like these simple fishermen did that night so long ago.

"Domine, Domine, salva nos—Lord, Lord, save us! We are perishing!" It sounds just like our cries, does it not? And lo and behold, the Master rose and calmed the raging sea. He relaxed the trembling occupants of that tiny boat, leaving them in bewilderment, in overwhelming amazement. "And there came a great calm." What a beautiful true story this is. Everyone should at one time or other read it in full. (Matthew 8: 23-27)

THIS EXPERIENCE OF THE BAPTISM IN THE SPIRIT AWAITS YOU. IN ESSENCE:

It is a religious experience.
It is a prayer experience.
It changes people into persons who now experience the risen Christ in a very exceptional and distinctive personal way. It is a release of an indwelling power sleeping within us as given to us when we received Baptism of water, and Confirmation (laying on of hands). We were given life on earth for a purpose.

As authentic visible signs to both self and to community, such an experience usually leads a person to an intense and personal deep devotional life. It deals first with the person himself or herself before sending them forth into the arena of valid evangelization, be this within one's home or with religious or civic associations. God Himself with the Holy Spirit will call and reveal Himself to different individuals "in measures" for His divine plan. (cf. to St. Paul, Ephesians 4: 7)

In addition, and very personally enriching, the baptism in the Holy Spirit continues to purify His human selected instruments by daily calling each of them to conversion, to repentance, to contrition, to a profound holy life. It offers power over sin and conquest over habits where struggles were once very persevering.

Once the Baptism in the Spirit is accepted, one gradually sees life in different but in truthful values, not in the greedy acquiescence of money; not in sex without love, without commitment; not in irrational evaluation of worldly commodities. All these, certainly, in their pure state, in their proper perspective, are gifts. The question, however, is how do we respect these gifts in utilizing them for our material needs and our spiritual welfare; how do we use them for and in the assistance of others while we still have some time to use them on this earthly passage from here into eternity where we will meet an honest judgment and a gracious reward.

A New Inner Power Bursts Forth:

EVERYBODY EVENTUALLY WANTS TO FIND A SIMPLICITY OF LIFE WHICH HELPS THEM TO COME CLOSER TO GOD. GREAT MEN AND WOMEN OF ALL TIMES ARE PERFECT EXAMPLES OF THIS. SUCH GREAT FIGURES AMONG A HOST OF MANY ARE HISTORICALLY RECORDED IN THE PERSONS OF SUCH FIGURES AS ST. FRANCIS, ST. IGNATIUS, OSWALD CHAMBERS, D.L. MOODY, ST. FRANCIS XAVIER, ST. CAMILLUS FOR THE SICK, CHARLES SPURGEON, ANDREW MURRAY, MOTHER TERESA, DOROTHY DAY, ST. BERNADETTE, ST. FR. PIO, ST. FAUSTINA.... SO, SO, SO MANY MANY MORE!

LIKE THESE ABOVE PERSONALITY EXAMPLES, A SOUL IN UNION WITH GOD HAS A THIRST FOR MORE UNION WITH THE ONE LOVED.

Such dispositions arise, crave and bask and give beneficial birth for and in a further attraction to a life of prayer, especially in the reading of sacred Scripture. If one belongs to a sacramental church community, then a hunger for and to the sacraments—those individual sacraments appropriately permitted, of course, according to one's chosen state of life, or for the spiritual condition of the moment. In feeding this spiritual life, one seeks for healthy balanced prayer meetings. From this inner life development and growth, there is born the desire to share and to perform good works, and other corporal works of mercy. This extends necessarily to healthy Godly behaviors in those various professional arenas built upon decent revealed dogmatic and moral principles. This outgoing behavior is authentic evangelization. It is Godly and Christian men and women through the use of charisma going into the arena of the world with the Good News of the Kingdom which our Blessed Lord fulfilled.

All these "wonders of wonders" serve as means to influence people lost in a darkened forest, or whatever, and to help them to remain in "the love" of Him who loved them without reservation. What a beautiful story of love this is! It is the adventure of God becoming man that man might become Godly.

In life's relationships, we try not to grieve another. Why? Because we can only grieve one who loves us. That is where the real deep pain lies. God loves us; and we grieve His love when we go away from Him through sin. Grieving is an act by which one rebukes, rejects, abandons another, leaving them almost hopeless. It destroys trust and belief. It leaves one a lonely wanderer.

PART FOUR

BAPTISM IN THE HOLY SPIRIT

GOING INTO THE ARENA OF THE WORLD: CALLED TO SERVE!

TRUE LOVE IS GOING OUT TO LEND A HELPING HAND:

"HE AIN'T HEAVY, FATHER, HE'S MY BROTHER."

Essentially, by the baptism of the Spirit, a person begins to know really the meaning of true love. It has within itself a force which leads to ways in expressing love for love; and this goes out into good service to others. It offers a helping hand: a bandage, medicine, opportunity to begin again, visiting the sick, the imprisoned, consoling the dying and caring for the elderly confined. You name it, and you will find the Divine Healer walking the long and lonely paths, roads, streets, homes and hospitals, the dark and silent fearful nights experienced by a thousand and a million souls who are wondering if this life was worth it at all.

They suffer the most anguishing pain of all as they ask themselves, "Why was I born? Where am I going? Was it worth it at all? Is there a God who really exists, who really cares?" In my healing ministry, these are real people who come for a touch of heaven's grace from souls who themselves are blessed in the Holy Spirit.

You, too, can be one of these agents of grace. In all this world, there is nothing more precious than believing and living the thought that "HAPPINESS IS FOUND WHERE I WILL BE NEEDED THE MOST."

CHRIST CALLS YOU; CHRIST NEEDS YOU:
You can be the incarnate continuation of the God who became visible so long ago but who lives now in, through, and with you. What a gift this is for you and for me! It is all ours, if we just take that grace. Our thoughts are His; our hands His; our feet His; our love His; our caress His! All that we share and give away is His continued living Presence—never dead.

What a marvelous story this is! In reality, it is "love service" performed in our personal way to God Himself who lives in that person whom we meet and who is crossing our path. It demonstrates itself as a camouflaged Divinity hidden beneath human flesh.

All This is The Social Gospel:
All authentic Godly and Christian Behavior must focal point itself into the social gospel. This means bringing God's blessings to mankind's needs.

In so doing, this leads to the social gospel of doing good for others who, due to some personal and sensitive experiences in life's journey, may be desperately groping in darkness or in need. This is evangelization at its authentic primary purpose. To visibly fulfill these good works, God thereupon gives men and women gifts—charisms in the Holy Spirit! (1 Corinthians 12)

The Experience in the Baptism of the Holy Spirit:

The experience in the Holy Spirit in effect means that a person's imagination, his or her reason, his or her will, emotions, whole person and being are now directed to God who touched them in this holy special personal way. It prepares them for service in the arena of their history and their life period in time.

A Promise Kept:

From that very first day of Pentecost when Jesus fulfilled His promise to send His Spirit to us, the good Master through the Holy Spirit has rounded persons from every time and century. He needed visible channels, Christians empowered with divine imparted gifts. He would guide them and send them out into all areas of the world, from their own little villages, towns, cities, countries— from their own families to the families of all races and creeds.

Jesus chose ordinary men in those first days of His assignment in establishing His Church. He equipped them for their distinctive mission. Each had a special job for a special place. The world was their arena. On that Pentecost Sunday, when our dear Lord sent the Holy Spirit, something totally unusual happened. It was a very strange phenomena, but it was exciting; it was joyful; it was powerful. The Holy Spirit changed the apostles' and the disciples' lives immediately and dramatically. He "imparted into" them power to perform unusual blessings. In reading Acts 2: 5 we see these baptized in the Spirit men go forth in the power of preaching and teaching, of producing healing miracles so as to confirm the message of the Gospel story. We see them cast out demons and speak in various languages.

Before one can preach and teach, they themselves must understand what they promulgate. And so, the Holy Spirit gave these leaders the marvelous gift of understanding (John 14: 26).

He strengthened them in their moments of trial and martyrdom by infusing in them the graces of comfort, guidance, and inspiration.

Can you with conjecture of thought and imagination place yourself there in Jerusalem on that day of Pentecost. Just think! Just imagine with a contemplation of mind. Suddenly there came a sound from heaven, like a mighty wind which seemed to fill the whole house, and it shook it to its foundations. Parted tongues of fire appeared and rested upon every one of them. It was the coming of the Holy Spirit.

Changed in the Spirit:
Immediately the Apostles and the Disciples
of the Lord underwent a new experience.
Suddenly, they realized that a change
overpowered them. Looking at themselves,
and observing each other's new behavior,
they realized that they became different
people. What was the change? Their minds
were enlightened; their hearts burned with a
fire of love. Extraordinary graces
permeated—inflamed them—in what
theologians call Charismata.

What were these graces? All graces from
God are synthesized in one word, and that is
love.

These graces enabled them to preach the
love story of Jesus and His Father
demonstrated through the Presence of the
Holy Spirit. Their preaching and their
teaching would be the proclamation of
uniting and identifying all hearers who
would accept the message to be other
Christs. Their proclamation, accompanied by
signs and wonders, would convince and
lead others to know, to love, and to serve
the love of Christ Jesus the Lord.

A World Set Aflame:
Strange and unusual events spread like
wildfire. News of the wonderful thing that
had happened in that Upper Room spread
rapidly like wildfire throughout the city, and
soon great crowds of people gathered
around the house.

Peter—From Weakness to Strength:

Peter, after his fall through his human weakness and his denial of Christ after having made many promises of loyalty, becomes with the absolution of Christ's forgiveness, a man for all seasons. Why this man to be chosen to be the Rock of Christ's Church? Peter—sanguine-tempered, from sinner to saint—steps out into the arena of the world as the first Pope. Boldly, confidently, Peter now stands tall and unafraid. Peter—Saint to be by his life in Christ and in his martyrdom of shed blood upon a wooden beam of a cross thrusted upside-down into the earth of Roman sands—stepped forth, with the other eleven apostles surrounding him. It is almost like the majestic balcony at St. Peter's Basilica in Rome.

What Does He Do?

He opened his human mouth—once having denied with that same mouth his Master and Lord—and freshly anointed in the Spirit of God, he breathes forth the powerful convincing message that the Christ who was crucified was indeed the Son of God. His message echoed vibrantly to the gathered multitude who had come from all parts of the world. Essentially his message was the convicting reminder to the hearers that all the prophesies of old which had been made concerning the Messiah, were now fulfilled. Peter, furthermore, showed how these prophecies had been completed in the Christ crucified.

That day of Pentecost was the day of all days! It was the birthday of the Christian Church. Evangelism at its best became born by a fisherman whose sandaled shoes would leave footsteps to follow into a world so much in need of a living savior.

The message was heard! The message for many did not fall upon ears which did not hear, nor into hearts which were closed; but that message, so longingly awaited, was received. The message was responded to with an enormous historical first century "altar call." That day—a day never to be forgotten—historically recorded three thousand souls as being added to the archives of the nascent Church.

A Story Worthy of Remembrance:
What a wonderful narration of truth this story imparts! Try to do some extra reading about the Nazarean who blessed with His sandaled footsteps the earthly sands of Palestine. Attempt to search and unfold the recordings of man throughout the past centuries of a Galilean who called men and women to follow His way and His truth.

Become acquainted with the Acts of the Apostles, as written recorded truth by a gentile doctor whose name was Luke, a medical doctor, who it is said learned about the Christ from St. Paul whom he served, loved and medically cared for. Read his accounts both in the Gospel of Luke as well as in the Acts of the Apostles. The enriching descriptive facts which also tradition tells us that he, Luke, himself learned from the holy Mother of God—the Virgin Mary.

Search the treasures of sacred readings! You will read, and you will find accurate complete history. True history books, if they are true history recordings, must also include, if they are not prejudiced to God and the Church, the historical facts of God's dealings in the affairs of mankind.

PART FIVE

RECEIVING THE BAPTISM IN THE HOLY SPIRIT

You are eligible -- everyone is.
God is a giver of gifts. But these gifts are so precious. Indeed, they are exceptionally powerful! The Heavenly Father Himself, with His infinite wisdom, discretely discerns the receiver and the recipient of graces so divine and so powerful before they are infused in human vessels of clay. He selects whom He wills. (Ephesians 4)

Loyalty: the broken clay of the potter.
The Almighty is concerned in our loyalty, even in spite of our human fickled attitudes. He smiles as He overlooks our frailties and our follies.

The Lord is patient and <u>persistently persistent</u> to call us to higher accountabilities, to walk and to swim into deeper waters of responsibilities, even if at times we frail creatures show inconstancies. Nevertheless, the Master's vision of insight knows that way down deep inside of His chosen men and women, there is our willingness to remain in His love regardless of our hard times or good times.

Our weaknesses become His raw material for His strength. With this raw material of our human nature, our personality, our temperament, He astonishingly confounds the proud, the worldly, the ambitious arrogance of pretentious persons.

God cannot use proud persons. Men and women, weak and broken, who may be the corner stones rejected by others, are generally the most eligible servants for the Master's work. Usually, these are people who when broken, tired, and humbled are they who in reality have dropped the pretentious mask for social acceptance. They are the personified power forces who are born for grandiose services both to God and to all mankind.

Something Wonderful:
Somehow, something wonderful happens at this point. People come to know that they are human creatures in need of a Savior who never lets them down, regardless of their frail condition.

They experience their weaknesses and their human poverty. Upon this humility, they find true power to grow. They come to the realization that the Creator produces His masterpieces of finest art from broken pieces, from broken glass, from broken lives which from here into eternity will always be our constant human companion. It is like the Old Testament story of the broken clay: "Like clay in the hand of the potter, so are you in My hand."   (Jeremiah 18: 6)

God is so very well noted for His working of marvelous wonders when He so often works through paradoxes. Have you noticed this?

PART SIX

RECEIVING THE BAPTISM IN THE HOLY SPIRIT

What must one do to receive the indwelling and the Baptism in the Holy Spirit?

There are some essential requirements.
Maybe we can call them Conditions.
As it is with service personnel, or with
exams in selecting candidates for
responsible duties, so it is with the Master
and Lord Jesus in His selecting trustful men
and women.

Some of these essentials are:

1- Faith in the promises of our Blessed Lord
   to receive the Baptism in the Holy Spirit

2- Repentance from all sin—personal and
   social

3- Sorrow for sin—hurting the one we love

4- **Desire to do better—justice and restoration**

5- **Desire to do as the Holy Spirit would direct, i.e. being open to the Spirit**

6- **Sharing with others—through words and deeds. This is the social gospel.**

7- **It can be received privately or publicly. The wind of the Spirit blows where it wills.**

PART SEVEN

LOVE
CALLS FOR LOVE

The old familiar Nelson Eddy song of <u>Indian Love Call</u> is so popularly apropos at this moment in attempting to receive the Baptism in the Holy Spirit.

To me personally, my attempt in leading you to the Baptism in the Holy Spirit as God's call of love to you is that you not only hear but unreservedly trust in surrendering yourself to this forceful power. God, who is love, and who creates and sustains mankind in His unchangeable love for you, can only call you through the heart of love. This call echoes from over the white chalked hills of Bethlehem of a baby cry to the manly cry of a Savior from the Cross planted in Calvary's hill, "Father, forgive them, for they know not what they do." (Luke 23: 34) This message embraces every white, every yellow, every red and black person, regardless of mankind's personal self-accommodating custom-made creeds.

God wants a family.
God wants rightly so His family of mankind.
God is on the move to do so.
God needs legionnaires—an army of believers with fire in their spirits, blood and not coca cola in their veins. He calls them to action, to a cause, the cause of all causes, the salvation of their souls. So many persons are lost in themselves, in their eventually betraying philosophies, their materialism, their secularism, their humanism—so many deceitful "isms." A voice needs to be delivered. A voice needs to be heard. A voice needs to be responded to. The price is high—very high! It deals with the loss of one's eternal soul.

God does not in my opinion "challenge" persons to the call. God, I believe, "invites" persons to the call of service. Oh, "To serve is to reign—servire regnare est!"
(Revelation 5: 10)

When you accept to be baptized in the Spirit, you are answering God's Love Call.
When you are baptized in the Holy Spirit, you become <u>identified</u> in and with Christ. This, however, is a different baptism than that with the Baptism in Water. This distinction is very important to clarify because many persons are not in this objective understanding.

When you are baptized in the Holy Spirit you are empowered with Charismatic Gifts <u>for a purpose</u> of serving the family of God. You do this in the local church communities, and you bring this power to the social world. You <u>influence</u> them; you don't push them into God. You leave their freedom of choice to themselves. God's grace through you and through the external and manifested experiences of the gifts, such as healing miracles, and others, will be launching paths for their thinking, and hopefully their own free surrender to the God of Love.

After God anoints you in the Presence and in the power of the Holy Spirit, He sends you forth with His and your unique spiritual gifts for the purpose of helping to spread the message of salvation. Regardless of what you may be, inadequate or not, broken or weak, sick or healthy, you can carry the gospel to imperfect persons by you yourself an imperfect person. Powerful and astounding is it to see the joy of imperfect persons like you and me, and many others, who can blend together to help call or to restore God's family.

PRAYER TO THE HOLY SPIRIT

Dear Holy Spirit,

In the sanctity of my baptized soul I have become a temple of Your Presence in me.

I accept You into my being, and I recognize You as the third Person of the Holy Trinity.

Cleanse my being from every sin, known or unknown, so that I may be a worthy dwelling place for You, dear Holy Spirit.

Cleanse my heart by the light of Your holy Presence. Enkindle in me the fire of Your flaming love.

Cleanse my thoughts by Your inpouring, and grant me the grace to love You perfectly, to praise You worthily, to serve You devotedly.

I give You my whole being. Enlighten me, guide me, strengthen me, console me. Tell me what to do, guide my free will according to Your divine will and plan. I surrender to You, and You only, the greatest gift I have, that being my free will.

Make Your decisions, my decisions. Direct my every choice. I promise to submit myself to all that You desire of me and to accept all that You permit to happen to me. I am trusting You with my life. Just stay close to me and help me to work with You when the cunning evils of the evil one deceptively attempt to possess my soul, and he continuously tries, restlessly, to separate me from You. How foolish he is because he knows that You are LORD, a name and title he cannot stand!

I praise You and I thank You for the joy of Your holy Presence.

So be it, Amen.

The Promise of the Spirit

"It shall come to pass in the last days, says God, that I will pour out a portion of My Spirit on all mankind. And your sons and daughters will prophesy, your old men will dream dreams, your young men will see visions. And even on the male and female servants I will pour out My Spirit in those days. And I will display wonders in the sky and on the earth."

(Joel 2: 28-30)

THE HOLY SPIRIT

IN

YOUR LIFE

THE SPOUSE OF YOUR SOUL

SUMMARY

THE FRUIT OF THE SPIRIT

WHAT THE SPIRIT IMPARTS TO US

THERE ARE EIGHT MAIN FRUIT OR EFFECTS FROM THE SPIRIT:

1- **LOVE**

2- **PEACE**

3- **PATIENCE**

4- **KINDNESS**

5- **GOODNESS**

6- **FAITHFULNESS**

7- **GENTLENESS**

8- **SELF-CONTROL**

THE GREATEST POWER
IN
THE WORLD

THE GREATEST POWER IN THE WORLD SPEAKS REALISTICALLY TO EVERYONE WHO NEEDS GOD TO TOUCH THEIR LIVES; AND THAT POWER IS WHAT JESUS PROMISED TO SEND AND TO CARRY OUT HIS MISSION. THAT POWER IS THE PERSON OF THE HOLY SPIRIT. HIS POWER IS THE GENTLE SENDER OF THE APOSTLES INTO TIME AND INTO ETERNITY. HE IS THE HEALING GRACE AND THE GENTLE POWER.

I TELL MY AUDIENCES TIME AND TIME AGAIN -- AND I ALSO NEED TO REPEAT THIS DAILY TO MY OWN SELF AS WELL -- THAT NONE OF US HAS TO GO DOWN IN DEFEAT. WE WERE NOT MADE FOR DEFEAT!

IT DOES NOT MATTER TO GOD WHAT WAS OR IS WRONG IN A PERSON'S LIFE, BODY, MIND, SPIRIT, OR SOUL. THE POWER OF GOD, THE HOLY SPIRIT, THE THIRD PERSON OF THE HOLY TRINITY, CAN AND WILL MAKE IT RIGHT IF WE ALLOW HIM TO DO SO.

EACH OF US HAS A LOVING FATHER, AND HE IS THE ALMIGHTY GOD!
HE IS OUR CREATOR, OUR STRENGTH, OUR LIFE, OUR BEGINNING AND OUR END. HE IS THE "ALPHA" AND THE "OMEGA" OF ALL CREATIONS.

THE HOLY SPIRIT HAS AN IRRESISTIBLE FORCE, AND HE MANIFESTS HIMSELF IN THOUSANDS OF MIRACULOUS HEALINGS, AND IN OTHER BLESSINGS.

I HOPE TODAY YOU WILL READ THESE CHAPTERS. JUST SIT. READ, REFLECT AND CONSIDER WITH CLEAR CLEAN THINKING, AND LISTEN TO THE VOICE OF THE LORD WHO SPEAKS TO US THROUGH THE SCRIPTURES, THROUGH THE CHURCH, THROUGH OUR CONSCIENCES, AND THROUGH CIRCUMSTANCES OF OUR LIVES.

ABSORB AND ASSIMILATE THESE THOUGHTS PRESENTED TO YOU.

I PRAY YOU THAT YOU WILL BE TOUCHED, BE MOVED BY SOME THOUGHT, OR SOMEONE'S NARRATED PERSONAL STORY. I BESEECH YOU TO HEAR AND SEE WHAT GOD HAS SPOKEN AND CAN DO. MAYBE IT MIGHT JUST BE A PRAYER -- WHATEVER! THEY MAY BE FOR YOU A SOURCE OF FREEDOM AND SAFETY FROM ANY OR WHATEVER MORTAL STORM CONFRONTS YOU.

THE HOLY SPIRIT WILL DO THIS. THE HOLY SPIRIT WANTS TO COMMUNICATE TO YOU. WILL YOU ANSWER? HIS MESSAGE IS VERY PRIVATE TO YOU. MAY YOU BE WILLING AND ATTENTIVE TO READ, THINK AND APPLY HIS MESSAGE OF TRUST, LOVE, AND POWER!

THERE IS NO GREATER GIFT THAN THAT OF TRUST AND LOVE. IT IS A TREMENDOUS POWER! AND THAT POWER OF TRUSTFUL LOVE IS THE HOLY SPIRIT!

**<u>GOD LOVE YOU,
   AND HEAL YOU !</u>**

Fr. Ralph A. DiOrio

The people He heals inevitably spread the word in supermarkets, in restaurants, at church, over coffee, while jogging, and through books such as this one. Their purpose is not to draw attention to themselves, but rather to focus your attention on God's love for each and every one of us.

Many years ago, as the story goes, a man named Jesus walked the earth spreading love, and ridding His Father's children of illness and disease. These miracles, or signs and wonders as they are also called, not only restored health but also turned doubters toward God.

HOLY SPIRIT CONCEPTS

HEALING RESTORATION:

Points of value for you:

Jeremiah 33: (1) 3-9/ Restoration of Jerusalem, etc.
Cure on the Sabbath.... John 5: 1-9

You and this book:
It is not by chance you have obtained this book; but God's love and divine providence have invited you to walk in the pathways beyond human expectation. You and the Holy Spirit are now on a voyage of revelation—a discovery of the most precious person of His creation—and that person is you.

The world awaits your entrance and your healing touch.

How wonderful it is for you to say, "Thank You, Lord. Send Thy Holy Spirit within me."

Why is God depending upon your "yes" to His invitation to walk into the arena of a hungry and thirsty world?

It is definitely a privilege for this book to speak to your heart, your soul, your spirit.

You are reading in this book word by word, sentence by sentence, paragraph by paragraph, chapter into chapter, into an inevitable gift to burst into a life which belongs to you, but for so many a day in your life you have remained a stranger.

Why you and the Spirit, working together? Because you are the answer to somebody's prayer. Somebody—relative, friend, a stranger who knows you from afar—has taken time out of the span of their life, and through sacrificial love just for you, whispered your name to the Almighty Throne of Heaven.

They prayed for you in what is known as the power of intercessory prayer!

LET US PRAY <u>RIGHT AWAY</u>—right from where you are!

In your silence of prayer, God speaks to your bursting heart. In this prayer, you come to know who you are, you come to realize who your God is, and because you know who you are and who God is, you come to know why you were born.

As you come to know your God, YOU KNOW WHO IS GOD. That's for sure! YOU KNOW WHAT GOD CAN DO! God is always God; and man always is man, but God uses man to visualize and factualize His love for you, for the world, and for me.

PRAYER:
LORD, PLEASE DO NOT ALLOW ANYONE OR ANYTHING TO STAND BETWEEN ME AND YOU.

JESUS, I DO BELIEVE IN YOU. I WANT YOU IN MY LIFE. PLEASE FORGIVE ME. WRITE MY NAME IN YOUR BOOK. I AM NOT ASHAMED TO REACH OUT TO YOU. HEAL ME WHEREVER I HURT. CONFIRM IN ME YOUR PRESENCE. GRANT ME WHAT ONLY YOU CAN GIVE AND DO WITH MY NORMAL HUMANITY. THAT IS, LORD, GRANT ME TODAY YOUR GIFT OF AN UNCOMMON PEACE, UNCOMMON JOY, UNCOMMON LOVE. I WANT TO LIVE IN YOUR LIFE. YOUR PRESENCE BECOMES MY OBSESSION. THUS LET ME SING WITH THE JOY WITHIN ME BECAUSE I AM IN YOUR PRESENCE.

THOUGHT: LOVE BEING IN THE PRESENCE OF THE LORD. GOD HAS AN UNCOMMON BLESSING FOR YOU. HE WILL TAKE—IF YOU LET HIM—YOUR COMMONNESS AND TURN IT INTO UNCOMMON MIRACLE LOVE. THEN THE ANGELS OF HEAVEN WILL BE AROUND YOU, YOUR FAMILY, YOUR HOME, YOUR ALL.

The fragrance and the holiness of the gift of joy and healing love rest in the welcoming of the <u>Holy Spirit in this house—your soul!</u>

POINTS FOR HEALING LOVE: <u>Write this down!</u>

But the Holy Spirit cannot come and dwell / nor heal you, if there are negative presences dwelling in you. Hell cannot live with heaven. DARKNESS CANNOT STAND THE LIGHT!

Some of these negative hindrances are:
- depression
- sadness
- envy
- pride
- hatred
- selfishness
- anger
- gluttony in all aspects
- covetousness
- murder in thought and in deed
- jealousy
- sloth
- BARGAINING WITH GOD - A LITTLE BIT FOR GOD AND A LOT FOR ME, etc.

ALL THESE REMOVE THE JOY OF HIS PRESENCE.
ALL THESE OR EVEN JUST SOME OR ONE PREVENT
HIS PRESENCE OF BLESSINGS.
HEALING CANNOT COME TO A SOUL FILLED WITH
DUPLICITY.

LET ME HELP YOU TO REMOVE SOME OR ALL OF THESE HINDRANCES.

SOME SCRIPTURAL CAUSES FOR HEALING LOVE FROM THE HOLY SPIRIT:

Medical doctors agree (a form of inner healing through analysis):

1- UNCONFESSED SIN:

God cannot let you encounter or receive the gift of the Holy Spirit which is Blessed Joy.

You cannot enter into joy if you are in defiance.

God will not allow you to disregard His Presence.

(Isaiah 59: 2)   "Rather it is your crimes that separate you from your God. It is your sins that make Him hide His face so that He will not hear you."

Your iniquities have separated you / deprived you all these years: i.e. greed for gain, making comparisons with others (jealousy), and thus having envy.

Remember! Whatever controls you—a person, or a thing—is your obsession; and it controls you!

For example: when you are criticized, you seem to go crazy. Then you even feel that there is nothing good in you, and for you, left.

Sometimes, something you say can offend the Holy Spirit; and the Holy Spirit will withdraw from you.

THUS: depression is the fruit, the consequence of His absence because in His Presence there is fullness of joy. (Ps. 60: 11 / 1-14) i.e. Lament after Defeat.

2- An **UNFORGIVING ATTITUDE or SPIRIT:**

An unforgiving attitude!

3- **IMPATIENCE** in waiting for Him to provide for something He promised.

4- **FATIGUE:** you need rest of body and spirit, and soul before you make good decisions.

WHAT TO DO:
TAKE IMMEDIATE ACTION:

Do not allow anyone or anything to enter into your soul. Be jealous of your soul.

Nobody can help you in the salvation of your soul. Only you, with God's grace, can victoriously reach salvation.

You have to get control and to get a hold on God, and reach for GOD!

For your problem, do not act as if it did not exist. Your mind will come apart, otherwise. And nothing will work for you. YOU WILL LOSE YOUR STRENGTH AND YOUR ENERGY WILL BE DEPLETED. THIS IS WHY WE FAIL TO OBTAIN ALL THE WONDERFUL PROMISES OF GOD.

WHAT TO PRACTICE FOR RESTORATION AND HEALING:

1- Respect for the Presence of God. Respect for His opinion. Read the word of God frequently / daily. Stay in and live in the word of God. CLEANSE YOUR MIND. YOU CANNOT HAVE A GREAT LIFE UNLESS YOU HAVE PURE LIFE, A PURE MIND.

2- HABITUALLY MEET WITH GOD FORMALLY / A TIME OF PRAYER DAILY! SANCTIFY A PLACE IN YOUR HOUSE V.G. LIKE A CHAPEL/ PRAYER ROOM. WELCOME YOUR FAMILY THERE. PRAY TOGETHER THERE. YOU AND YOUR FAMILY WILL GAIN. YOU WILL ALWAYS THEN BE SAFE. JUST YOU AND YOUR GOD. DISCUSS EVERYTHING WITH HIM IN A SIMPLE FEELING WAY. (I DID ABOUT MY CROSS: LOST, AND FOUND THROUGH A DREAM.)

3- TALK YOUR EXPECTATIONS INSTEAD OF YOUR EXPERIENCES. WORDS EXPRESS WELL WHO AND WHAT YOU ARE ALL ABOUT. GOD GAVE YOU A GOOD MIND; AND HE GAVE YOU A GOOD TONGUE TO SPEAK, TO TALK IT OUT. (PENCIL AND PAPER)

THUS! IT IS WISDOM THAT YOU ARE ASKING FOR. AND IT IS WISDOM WHICH CAN AND WILL CHANGE YOUR LIFE.

(cf. REFER TO PRAYER FOR WISDOM DIVINE.)

TO THE SICK AND THE SUFFERING
who are always among us, we offer our privilege to serve. May everyone who reads these stories come to the Lord refreshed and restored. May their hope for the future become the faith of the present.

SECTION V

Listen
To
My Story

We turn to You, O God of every nation, Giver of life and origin of good. Your love is at the heart of all creation. Your hurt is people's broken brotherhood.

"The biggest disease today is not leprosy or tuberculosis, but rather the feeling of being unwanted, uncared for and deserted by everybody. The greatest evil is the lack of love and charity, the terrible indifference toward one's neighbor who lives at the roadside assaulted by exploitation, corruption, poverty and disease."

~Mother Teresa of Calcutta

"HEAL US, O LORD, AND BRING US TOGETHER"

Dear Blessed Lord, You are the giver of all good things; You are the source of every blessing. You call all peoples, all individuals, to be one in You and in each other. You give us the grace of holy and human compassion for every broken and wounded individual whom life permits to cross our daily paths.

To see You, dear Lord, in them it is so very necessary that You send into each one of us Your Holy Spirit. May this Holy Spirit give us the insight, the courage, and the strength to truly embrace Your continued wounds and scars in suffering humanity.

May Your healing love penetrate our beings; let it prepare our hearts to receive and to embrace You as we embrace and receive any human person regardless of race or creed, sinner or saint.

As a token of Your pleasure and gratitude, gift us, as You are the Giver of gifts, with gratitude for Your abiding Presence. Grant to all of us—especially to me—Your peace, Your joy, and the fullness of Your life dwelling in Your people. Amen.

Deidre Hall ministering to a sick infant

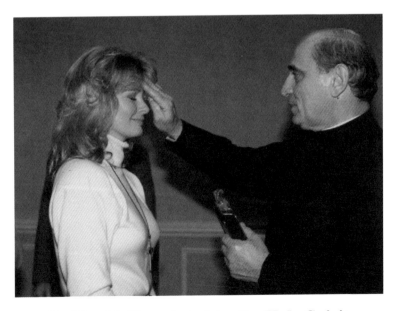

Deidre Hall anointed in the Holy Spirit

In Loving We Serve

The Divine Love Call is to serve the call of love from the cries of a broken and needful humanity.

To love is to serve—to serve is to reign.

A soul in union with God always has something to give.

Happiness is found where each person is needed the most. How very true this psychological and ethical statement is for each and every human being who walks across the breast of earth.

Every man, every woman, every youth, each and every person existing in the age of wisdom is called to share their presence in the life of another human being.

With gratitude to my dear actress friend, Deidre Hall from Hollywood, California. I am deeply appreciative that she has authorized me to utilize two of her photographs taken at one of my healing services in Leominster, Massachusetts. In these photos you will see how each and every person in the world, regardless of the multiple and burdensome tasks of each day's work, can always find the open door to love—to pray—and to heal another human being. Such is the expression of these two photos in which our dear friend, Deidre Hall, April 7, 1991, took time to come—to feel—to bring the healing gift of gifts—the gift of love and healing. You too—in whatever walk of life you travel—can find a living soul in need of the compassionate love of touch for a soul such as yours in union with God.

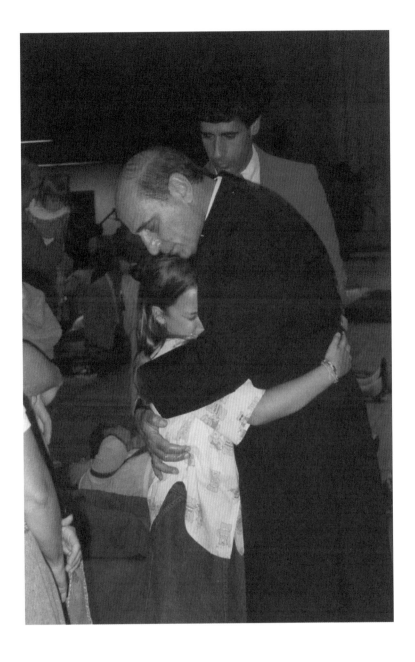

Seven Magnificent True Stories

which will undoubtedly embrace your
heart – stories which you will never
forget!

Read and Embrace
for your own precious needs how

The Everlasting Almighty Lover

remains for you and for me

The Divine Merciful Healer.

" I Have Loved You With An Everlasting Love. "

" He has taken me to the banquet hall, and His banner
over me is love."

Song of Songs 2:4

A SECRETARY'S INSIGHT

It is such a joy for me to introduce to you this first of a series of special testimonial accounts of the wonderful people who have tasted the agony of poignant suffering like never before and searched for a miracle, that drew them to experience God's loving mercy through the ministry of The Apostolate of Divine Mercy and Healing.

Each testimony of the "Magnificent Seven" is truly unique and inspiring. Their encounter with Our Loving and Merciful God transformed their lives forever. You will appreciate each person's life and the answer to their prayer. Yes, it all began with a prayer. Each person which you will be reading about willingly opened their hearts to you to share with you the indescribable joy of the Master's loving touch. Walk with them in gratitude and allow your faith to be strengthened and renewed in our living Lord.

Aldona M. Sarkauskas, CMA
Confidential and Personal
Secretary to Father Ralph A. DiOrio

My Prayer of Faith and Trust In My Living God

Lord, You are continuously trying to communicate with us. You respect our bodies, but nothing is more important to You than our souls. What a wonderful God You are!

Dear Lord, how very true it is that when a soul is in union with You, there is always a splendid springtime. Because of this belief and this trust, how very true it is that when You heal me in spirit, in soul, or in my body, I fully realize the value You have placed upon my human existence.

I thank You for not leaving us earthly mortals orphans. You always find a way to make Yourself visibly present. You send us wonderful persons— men and women, consecrated or lay persons, who enrich our lives with Your anointing Holy Spirit.

Through Your priestly servant, Fr. Ralph A. DiOrio, I came to know You—Your precious divine love. I truly accepted Your life into mine. Thank You, dear Lord, for introducing me to higher values, higher responsibilities, and not fearful to walk into deeper waters.

Because of this renewed Christian vitality, I even pray differently now. It has improved my daily existence. Every aspect of my life seems brighter, clearer.

My grateful heart simply wants to sing out Your praises. In gratitude I rededicate my remaining earthly life to You and Your cause. Please continue to live within me to continue living within You. I praise and glorify You. Amen.

Marc Pelosi

A Child's Heart Restored

Marc Pelosi

*"God, who made the world, and all things therein;
He, being Lord of heaven and earth, dwelleth not
in temples made with hands;*

*Neither is He served with men's hands, as
though He needed any thing; seeing it is He who
giveth to all life, and breath, and all things:*

*And hath made of one, all mankind, to dwell
upon the whole face of the earth, determining
appointed times, and the limits of their habitation.*

*That they should seek God, if happily they may
feel after Him or find Him, although He be not
far from every one of us:*

*For in Him we live, and move, and are; as some
also of your own poets said: For we are also His
offspring."*

(Acts 17: 24-28)

A Child's Heart Restored

Introduction by his mother Linda:

Not a day goes by that I don't thank God for the gift that He has given my family. Not only did He send us a gift of healing for our son, He gave our family new life. We now see the power of the Living God every day of our lives. I would not only like to extend a heartfelt thanks to Father DiOrio and The Apostolate of Divine Mercy and Healing for being the instrument through whom God uses to give us hope, but also to many of those who have continuously prayed for Marc and our family. The prayers of those whom I know and I don't know have been an integral part of my healing, hope and strength. Miracles do happen and with prayer, anything is possible. May God bless you and touch you as we have been touched.

Testimony by Linda Pelosi, mother of Marc.

Please let me introduce myself—my name is Linda Pelosi and I am a housewife with 3 children, ages 11, 10 and 3. I would like to share with you my experience attending your Healing Mass on March 18, 2001 in Sturbridge, MA. I learned of your ministry through a friend of mine, Arlene Dolce, who experienced several miracles, one of which you had a Word of Knowledge.

At the present time, Marc is two and a half years old. He will be three on November 9, 2003. We were told not to expect him to live to see his first birthday.

Marc's first blessing was on March 17, 2001. At that time, he had three heart conditions:
(1) Pulmonary Stenosis,
(2) HCM Hypertrophic Cardiomyopathy,
(3) Mitral Regurgitation.
The HCM is the serious one, the one which was supposed to take Marc's life. The Pulmonary Stenosis is the one that turned around and reversed itself after the first blessing. I testified to that in July 2001, the second blessing. Also, there was a thickness not only in Marc's left ventricle but in the right side, too, which thinned out and at that point Dr. Messina had told us that sometimes, just sometimes this could happen and then the left ventricle takes over. In other words, the right side

decreased but so the left side will continue to thicken to the point where it will throw the ventricle into an irregular heartbeat which would cause Marc to die. When Dr. Messina told us the right side had "melted away" we knew that it wasn't just something that happened. It was part of Marc's progressive healing.

After the July 2001 blessing, Marc's EKG in November, a few days after his first birthday, looked "just about normal." Which means it looked like any child's EKG would; there was a dramatic change from his previous EKGs. It wasn't until the echocardiogram in September of 2002 that showed the thickness in Marc's left ventricle decreased by 50%. This was a significant sign that showed Marc's heart condition was reversing itself and this is when I told Dr. Messina our story.

As of June 3, 2003, there was no echocardiogram taken. That will be in September 2003. Marc's EKG showed that everything looked well. He is still on medication; however, I did ask Dr. Messina if he would take Marc off of medication should he see the ventricle thinned out to normal and he said he had no problem doing that, "....when his heart healed."

I asked Dr. Messina about Marc's mitral leak and he said he is not worried about that because he would fix it if need be, but there is no need for that. (At which time we all are saying if God is healing the major problem he will heal it all). The only thing that was life threatening was the thickness in the left ventricle.

Dr. John Messina with Marc

This is Dr. John Messina's letter to Fr. DiOrio

Dear Father:

Re: Marc Pelosi

Mrs. Linda Pelosi asked me to drop you a correspondence regarding her son, Marc. This young boy was born with a very severe heart defect. The prognosis at the time was very poor, and many of these children do not survive. Marc has, however beaten the odds to date; he is two years old now and his heart disease is resolving over time. Although we are continuing to follow him, closely, we have an optimistic outlook about him.

Marc's mother would like me to extend this letter to you to let you know how well he is doing.

Thank you very much and God bless the great work that you do.

Sincerely,

John Messina, M.D., Chief
Division of Pediatric Cardiology

Prayer:

Lord and Savior Jesus, You are the personification of God's Divine Mercy, God's Divine Compassion. In God's love for His people, God has never left us orphans. And though many times, Lord, we in our humanity walk many darkened forests, we come out of these forests of human life in brokenness and tiredness and weariness, and we search for the light-- the light of a restoration in our humanity and a reunification of our brotherhood, the human family.

Lord Jesus, today by a special invitation, because of our own weaknesses and sicknesses, we have answered Your call to come to the Divine Mercy, and to receive the imparting of the resting of God's hands upon our broken humanity to give us the Divine Mercy of healing. Look into each heart here, Lord—those of us who come from different denominations, different ethnic groups— teach us to come beneath the Cross of Your Son, Jesus, and to receive the "sting" of love, the bloody scars of Him who went to Calvary's heights to give us the victory of an Easter healing. We give You all the praise and the glory!

Alexandra Saieh

An Aspiring Young Lady With A Dream

Alexandra Saieh

"Arise, be enlightened, O Jerusalem: for thy light is come, and the glory of the Lord is risen upon thee.

For behold darkness shall cover the earth, and a mist the people: but the Lord shall arise upon thee, and His glory shall be seen upon thee.

And the Gentiles shall walk in thy light, and kings in the brightness of thy rising.

Lift up thy eyes round about, and see: all these are gathered together, they are come to thee: thy sons shall come from afar, and thy daughters shall rise up at thy side.

Thou shalt no more have the sun for thy light by day, neither shall the brightness of the moon enlighten thee: but the Lord shall be unto thee for an everlasting light, and thy God for thy glory."

(Isaias 60: 1-4, 19)

An Aspiring Young Lady With A Dream

When we are faced with a problem in our lives (whether it be a health problem, family problem, etc.) we need to find the strength within ourselves to overcome it. Prayer is one of the most powerful ways to communicate with God. Prayer gives us the strength we need to overcome any difficulties we have in life. By praying to God, we have hope and God gives us His love in return.

Dear Father DiOrio,

I would like to give full testimony to your office of my healing because it has already been 13 years since I attended your healing service in Victoria. I was diagnosed with a brain tumor (astrocytoma) and I had to undergo surgery right away because the tumor had grown too deep into the brain. The surgeon could not remove the entire tumor so I had to receive radiation therapy at M.D. Anderson Cancer Center.

When I came back to Corpus Christi, I attended your healing service in Victoria, TX. Through the Holy Spirit, you described me and you said that I was going to receive the healing that day.

You also called me by my middle name, Katrina. I went to your Altar and you blessed me with holy oil and I felt very warm. I knew I was being healed at that moment. When that occurred, I was 13 years old. Thanks to your healing, I was able to finish High School and obtain a Bachelor's degree in Advertising from the University of Texas in Austin. I am now 27 years old and I currently live in Corpus Christi.

I am very grateful to you Father DiOrio and may God bless you always so you can continue your great Apostolate and services. We are a family from Colombia, South America and my father is a medical doctor. According to my dad, my case is a miracle. Thank you for your kindness and your prayers. With love from Alexandra and the entire Saieh family.

Prayer:

Father, anoint our minds today; anoint our souls; anoint our ears that they may hear Your Word; anoint our lips, Lord Jesus, that we may sing praises to You and pray from our hearts; anoint our hearts, dear Lord Jesus,

with Your love. Jesus, we come before You today, Lord Jesus...Heavenly Father, there are so many people here who have come with an expectant faith, believing that You truly keep Your word, that if we only believe without doubt, without any uncertainty, You will fulfill Your promises—Your promises of the great covenant from the Cross.

Heavenly Father, we bring all forms of brokenness of our humanity; we bring the destiny of our call to Eternal Life. And Jesus, before that moment of the lapse of our age passes on in time into eternity, we will appropriate Your promise of healing--healing in spirit, soul and body. Today, Lord Jesus, because we believe with expectant faith, all of us will receive the miracle of Your promise. And Lord, we will also understand the basis of healing among the steps to healing divine: that once we receive Your Presence of healing, our lives are no longer our own, but are for Your glory, and Your service, and Your commission, to build up the body of Christ. Mother of Jesus, Queen and Mother of the sick, pray for us. Good St. Anne, pray for us. St. Raphael, Archangel of journey, of love, and of healing, pray for us. Amen.

Bob Chamberland

Confident In The Promises Of God

Bob Chamberland

"Being justified therefore by faith, let us have peace with God, through our Lord Jesus Christ:

By whom also we have access through faith into this grace, wherein we stand, and glory in the hope of the glory of the sons of God.

And not only so; but we glory also in tribulations, knowing that tribulation worketh patience;

And patience trial; and trial hope;

And hope confounded not: because the charity of God is poured forth in our hearts, by the Holy Ghost, who is given to us."

(Romans 5: 1-5)

Confident In The Promises Of God

Since my October 2002 healing, it is clear to me that the Holy Trinity works through Father DiOrio. Every day I thank God for willing this gift of healing, Jesus for His sacrifice, and the Holy Spirit for the strength that I needed to cope with pain and granting me the gifts of love and forgiveness. All three came together when Father DiOrio laid hands on me.

I am in awe as to how much Jesus loves us and helps us everyday. It's all very simple. Believe in Jesus. Jesus is always here to help you. All you have to do is include Him in your life and ask for His help and guidance. Jesus will never forsake you. He embraces your burdens because it empowers the sacrifice that He made for you. All you have to do is lay your burdens at the foot of His Cross and accept Him as your Savior.

I, Robert J. Chamberland, am here to testify that Jesus heals through Father DiOrio. Here is my story.

On November 1, 1994, in one second, my whole
life changed. A driver going at least 50 MPH rear-
ended my car as I slowed down to allow the driver in
front of me to make a right turn. My car was totaled
and I was left with severe chronic neck and lower
back pain, which was diagnosed as myofascial pain
syndrome. On a scale of 1 - 10, my pain was
diagnosed as an 8/9, 10 being when I would pass out
from pain. I could no longer work and became
disabled. For the next 8 years, my pain was managed
with strong pain medication that had unpleasant side
effects.

On October 6, 2002, in one second, my whole life
changed again. I attended a healing service here in
Sturbridge, MA. (One of a few that I attended in the
last year and a half.) When Father DiOrio
approached me during the anointing with oil, I said,
"Father, I am ready for a miracle." Father asked me
what was wrong and I answered, "Severe neck and
back pain." Father asked, "From an automobile
accident?" I replied, "Yes." Father then laid his hands
on my chest and back. I was slain in the spirit. While
I was on the floor, I was in terrible pain and a voice
said, "Let it go." The voice again said sternly, "Let
go!" several more times. My pain left me. I got up
and Father later came to me and asked me, "How do
you feel? You've been healed!" I answered Father

DiOrio, "I have NO pain." I still have NO pain. Please, don't give up on your faith. Trust Jesus. Praise Jesus. Amen.

"And Jesus answering, said to them, 'Amen, I say to you, if you shall have faith, and stagger not, not only this of the fig tree shall you do, but also if you shall say to this mountain, 'Take up and cast thyself into the sea,' it shall be done.

And all things whatsoever you shall ask in prayer, believing, you shall receive.' "

(Matthew 21: 21-22)

Joseph McDonald

The Unimaginable Came True

Joseph McDonald and His Wife Judy

"Amen, amen I say to you: if you ask the Father any thing in My Name, He will give it you.

Hitherto you have not asked any thing in My Name. Ask, and you shall receive; that your joy may be full.

These things I have spoken to you, that in Me you may have peace. In the world you shall have distress: but have confidence, I have overcome the world."

(John 16: 23-24, 33)

The Unimaginable Came True

I would like to share my story from the two of us. If it weren't for my wife Judy's encouragement, I would have never gone to see Father DiOrio. This was something we handled together and here is my story.

Ten years ago, my world, as I knew it, changed. I was diagnosed with a rare from of cancer which had a poor prognosis. I wanted to keep this information private because I didn't want anyone to know; however, my wife had a different plan. She said we had to tell everyone we knew about my illness so that they could pray for me. My wife is a nurse and knew that I would need a miracle to be cured. We both got down on our knees and prayed. We prayed for a healing miracle and our prayers were answered. Our prayers were answered in many ways; through the love of our family and friends, the prayers of people we hardly knew and of course our visit to Father DiOrio.

I was depressed about the cancer and fatigued from the radiation treatment - the last thing I wanted to do was to travel to another state to visit a priest. My wife convinced me to go and said that it was her belief that if Father DiOrio touched me during the healing service, it was a sign from God that I was healed. How could I refuse?

I went to Father DiOrio's Healing Mass ten years ago. There were about one thousand people at the service and Father DiOrio touched only a few people that day and I was one of them. My wife's prayers were answered. She had no doubt that I had a healing miracle. Father DiOrio's words have never left me; he said, "Healing is the easy part; having the faith to believe is the tough part." My life changed that day; I did believe that I was healed. The doctors were less willing to believe in miracles, but after years of check-ups and testing, my doctor said, "I think you are cured."

For anyone who is living with a serious illness, I hope you are blessed with a partner that has a strong faith and the hope to take the leap of faith and put yourself in God's Hands and believe in miracles.

"In the beginning was the Word, and the Word was with God, and the Word was God. The same was in the beginning with God. All things were made by Him, and without Him was made nothing that was made. In Him was life, and the life was the light of men. And the light shineth in darkness, and the darkness did not comprehend it." (John 1)

Thought for Reflection:

God is light, and you and I have been walking in a thousand and one different darknesses. And this is the sadness of you and me--when things are going pretty well, we forget God. But when there's trouble and aches and pains and sufferings, then we run to God. How sad it is to live outside of God's light. How sad it is to put material objects ahead of God. We have lost values in our existence...we have lost the light. Those of us who are looking for light always end up in darkness when we turn the light away from us--the light is still there.

Although He made the world, the world did not recognize Him when He came. Only a few would welcome and receive Him, but to all who received Him He gave the right to become children of God.

Do you realize the inheritance that you received from God? It's an opportunity today to recognize that beautiful gift.

As long as you're on this side of heaven's eternity, God will always give you another opportunity, another second, another minute.

Joan Catherine Wise

She Was Enraptured In Awe Of Her Savior

Joan Catherine Wise

"For God is my witness, whom I serve in my spirit in the gospel of His Son, that without ceasing I make a commemoration of you;

Always in my prayers making request, if by any means now at length I may have a prosperous journey, by the will of God, to come unto you.

That is to say, that I may be comforted together in you, by that which is common to us both, your faith and mine."

(Romans 1: 9-12)

She Was Enraptured In Awe Of Her Savior

There is not one prayer that I have prayed that my God has not answered. He does not always answer my prayers in the way I wish, or I think would be ideal. He answers them according to His will, His purpose and through His wisdom. Life is a walk of trials and tribulations that takes me on a path of growth and changes. God uses every opportunity to capture my heart, to see Him in new ways and grow my faith. My vision of God is limited, but He orchestrates every situation in my life to see His glory, power and love—if I am so willing to look. My hope grows from the multitude of events in which I allow God to show me His mighty Hand. Allow God to take you on a path where you have never walked before to see the beauty of His love and the beauty of His kingdom.

Here is my story:

I was a manager of a vitamin store in Amsterdam, New York. About five miles from the mall is a shrine where priests come to seek the Lord and find a time of rest. One day while I was stocking my shelves, a priest came to the store and quietly looked over the vitamins for about an hour. I asked him twice if he needed help and he said no. The next day, the priest once again came to the store and looked around again for about half an hour. I asked him if he needed help and this time he said yes. He purchased numerous vitamins and when completing his order I noticed there were two items I did not have. I asked him if I could mail him the items when they were shipped to me and he politely agreed.

I took a pen and paper and asked him if he would write down his name and address so that I could mail him the items. He filled out the paperwork, paid for his order and slowly walked away to a pharmacy store to continue his shopping. I took the paperwork and looked down at his name and noticed it was DiOrio, with his address in Boston. I knew very well that there was a Father DiOrio who ministered the gift of healing, and he was from Boston. Since I was the only one on duty, I waited for about 20 minutes until my worker came in and told her that I needed to run over to the pharmacy for a minute. I then ran over to the store and tracked Father DiOrio down.

When I found him, I asked him if he was the priest with the gift of healing and he said yes. I then told him that he could not leave the mall without first praying for me. He said he would, handed me his vitamin bags and said he would come over in a little while.

Father DiOrio kept his word and returned in about half an hour. He came over to me, anointed me with oil, and asked me what I would like prayer for. I told him my church background (brought up Catholic and now serving God in a non-denominational church) and then explained that I was unable to have children. I also told him that my heart was to serve the Lord. He silently prayed for me, took his vitamins and left. Two weeks later, I mailed him his vitamins and wrote him a little note of thanks. He returned my thanks with a short note.

My life has never been the same. I now have two children, found the beauty of my Church heritage and have been able to incorporate my Catholic roots with my evangelical training to find a rich and deep understanding of Christ. God not only heard my prayers and saw my pain (as I was in an abusive marriage); He blessed me abundantly. You know what my original plan for college was—for a two-year degree to be a dental hygienist–God's plan for me was to be a doctor!

I believe, with all of my heart, that Father DiOrio's prayer for me was timely. I also believe there are two important points to be learned from my story. One, never let an opportunity of God pass by. And two, the power of prayer can change your life forever.

Oh, by the way, all those vitamins he bought? They were gifts for his secretaries! He had been traveling and wanted to bring them back something for all of their service and hard work they do for him. Father DiOrio was a humble, blessed, man of God!

Prayer:

Lord and Savior Jesus, I come before You as Your Priest; I come before You as Your Messenger of the gospel of hope, of healing. I thank You for the privilege of my call to serve—for in serving, Lord Jesus, each one of us reigns as we live for You and for others.

Grant, dear Lord, that those of us who have made this journey in pilgrimage to this, Your shrine of healing love, may obtain the blessings of Your Holy Spirit, that they may receive today drops from Your Precious shed Blood for us...Let me talk like You, Lord Jesus; let me love like You, Jesus; let me touch, embrace and heal as I see the broken body of You, Jesus, in these sick people, in these broken hearts, broken spirits.

We give You all the praise, Lord Jesus, You who are the Son of God. We praise You, Heavenly Father; we glorify You. We glorify the Holy Spirit who continues to sanctify us.

Mother of Jesus, pray for us. Mother, Help of the Sick, pray for us. Heart of Jesus...Jesus, I trust in You. Amen.

Andres Ramirez

My Cry Was Heard By The Master

Andres Ramirez

"Whosoever believeth that Jesus is the Christ is born of God. And every one that loveth Him who begot, loveth him also who is born of Him.

In this we know that we love the children of God: when we love God, and keep His commandments.

For this is the charity of God, that we keep His commandments: and His commandments are not heavy.

For whatsoever is born of God, overcometh the world: and this is the victory which overcometh the world, our faith."

(1 John 5: 1-4)

My Cry Was Heard By The Master

My name is Xann Ramirez and this is a brief story about my son, Andres Rosalio.

My husband Rene and I waited some time before we decided to have children so that we would be able to provide good things for whomever we brought into the world. The time came when we decided to try for a child and we had a hard time conceiving. We both prayed very hard and constantly and before we knew it, we were going to be parents. Andres came into the world on Mother's Day 2002 making us deliriously happy.

Everything was going so well until he reached about 5 months of age when I noticed a small knot on his right side. I didn't think much of it until it grew the size of a 1/2 dollar and was protruding. In December he was scheduled for surgery. The surgeon saw him and put it off until January. He had the January surgery, the mass removed and 6 weeks later came back clear cell sarcoma of the soft tissue. It was an extremely rare and terminal cancer. More scans were immediately done revealing strange formations in his abdomen; the thought was the cancer was in his gut. This whole time, Andres was growing on target, happy, and what appeared to be as thriving.

Surgery was scheduled for the following week to hopefully remove and identify further this abnormality. That night in desperation, I called looking for Father Ralph hoping someone would take my call out of what I figured was just one of hundreds in a day with hopeless cases just like my family's. I ended up on the other line with Aldona who was a complete God-send that prayed with me for the longest time, reassured me, and gave me strength when I had none of my own. My son's name was placed on Father Ralph's Altar and prayed for. The next morning the surgery took place and absolutely nothing was found at all. I never in my life thanked Jesus so much for taking care of my baby.

In the months after that, my son would get very ill once, pull through that, and then have a third surgery to go back to the original site of the tumor removed to a deep tissue excision to see if there were any cancer cells active. The results came back negative. He had no cancer cells and his CAT scans looked good. My son was given the best news possible and hope for the future. I truly feel that I owe this to Fr. Ralph delivering the healing power of God to my son thousands of miles away.

We are still having him remain under a very watchful eye of the doctors but I just keep my prayers going that God continues to provide a future for my son and give the doctors positive guidance to help us through this. We are very happy and forever praise this miracle because that is all my son is.... a miracle.

Prayer:

Thank you, Lord Jesus, for bringing us together today. We've been trying hard, Lord, to find our way out of the dungeon of darkness. May Your name be praised and worshipped today and glorified as we worship You, God—this is our primary purpose to be here today—to worship You, Creator, that having worshipped You, the doors and the windows of our lives are open to receive the fresh air of a fresh anointing: the anointing of Your Holy Spirit.

Mother of Jesus, thank you for saying ADSUM: "I will, I am here," when you answered the Angel's request in the name of God the Father: "Give Me a son. Give Me a son that you will raise and prepare for the sacrifice and the salvation of My people." Thank you, Mother Mary.

Stay close to us today, Mother Mary. And being our mother, clean our wounds, wash the dirt away. Give us clarity of mind; trust, as Jonah trusted God when he went into the belly of the whale; give us understanding in our sufferings as Job sought understanding;

and give us, yes, give us submission through the brokenness of our humanity as Jesus was in the Garden of Gethsemane. Give us the grace today, Lord Jesus, of being healed upon these truths and upon the fact that we know who we are and what we can do with our lives with Your grace. Amen.

Maddy Miller

Rejoicing In God My Savior

Maddy Miller

"I will praise Thee, O Lord, with my whole heart; in the council of the just, and in the congregation.

Great are the works of the Lord: sought out according to all His wills. His work is praise and magnificence; and His justice continueth for ever and ever.

He hath made a remembrance of His wonderful works, being a merciful and gracious Lord; He hath given food to them that fear Him. He will be mindful for ever of His covenant: He will shew forth to His people the power of His works.

That He may give them the inheritance of the Gentiles; the works of His hands are truth and judgment. All His commandments are faithful: confirmed forever and ever, made in truth and equity. He hath sent redemption to His people: He hath commanded His covenant for ever.

Holy and terrible is His name: the fear of the Lord is the beginning of wisdom. A good understanding to all that do it: His praise continueth for ever and ever."

(Psalm 110)

Rejoicing In God My Savior

On March 18, 2001, my life as I knew it had come to a screeching halt.

My friend's mother suggested that we attend one of Father Ralph's healing services in Sturbridge, Massachusetts. She has a neurological disorder which impedes her ability to walk and she is in constant pain. She asked if I wouldn't mind driving. Naturally, I was happy to oblige. One week later, my Mom and I along with my friend and her mother set out on our journey. We were going to take a nice leisurely ride up and spend a wonderful day together. Little did I know that her simple request would prove to be a dramatic life changing experience for me.

My only concern at the time was to see my friend's mother completely healed. Of course I never thought that I needed a healing. After all, I had my health, a wonderful husband and a thriving career as a news producer for a major network. With the usual disappointments and sorrows one must endure during the course of life, mine were not exceptional to basic human experience. Therefore, in the scheme of things, I thought everything in my life was under control. **Nothing could have been further from the truth.** Raised as a Roman Catholic, I did believe in God. However, there were a few things I didn't know.

For instance, I didn't know that there is a supernatural joy which can transcend every trial and tribulation life has to offer. I didn't know that inner peace produces total healing of mind, body and soul. I didn't know where my soul was going after my death. I didn't know that the only thing I needed most in my life was a personal relationship with Jesus Christ. And I didn't know that the events leading up to that revelation were going to be so incredibly powerful.

The second we arrived at Father Ralph's service, a sense of peace came over me. During the next few hours, Father spoke about God's infinite love and mercy. He constantly reassured us that no matter what sins we committed, God was there to forgive us. All we had to do was ask Him. It was a beautiful experience. You could feel the love in the room as we sang songs, held each other and prayed. Some cried, some laughed but it was apparent that everyone there was touched in a very special way. I had a wonderful feeling of happiness and the time just flew by.

Towards the end of the service, Father had an altar call for people who wanted to receive a blessing. Naturally, all four of us got in line and patiently waited our turn. Father was about to bless me when I asked him to anoint me as well. Since I appeared to be in good physical condition, he wanted to know why I requested the oil. I started to cry and said, "To heal my soul." With a gentle nod, he acquiesced. Father anointed my head with oil, and I heard him ask Jesus to take my soul. Suddenly as if I were hit with a ton of bricks, I fell backwards to the ground, surrounded by this glorious feeling of peaceful rest. There I was, on the floor in a semiconscious state, unable to move and weeping uncontrollably. It was as if the floodgates of my soul were opened and all the hurts, the pains and the sins seemed to pour out from me. I felt as though I was being cleansed.

What happened next was by far the most miraculous occurrence. I heard a soft, gentle voice say to me, "I am with you." I just knew it was Jesus. I sobbed some more and let out a big sigh of relief. I don't know how long I was out, but I do know this; the moment I got to my feet, I knew that I had a spiritual encounter with God. I was completely transformed and I felt as pure as the driven snow.

From that day forward, nothing was ever the same. I had such a desire to forgive all the people in my life who hurt me and just love them. What they did and what was done in the past, didn't matter anymore. What mattered is that Jesus loves me, forgave me and changed my heart. In that very instant, I turned my life over to Him. The only desire that I have now is to please Him and do His work. I see things differently. Much the same way a loving father looks at his children. I have more patience and understanding. I'm more readily able to forgive and I try to live a life that would make Jesus happy. I desire to be with those who love the Lord. I want to help hurting people and reach out to them with all the love that God has placed in my heart. I want to talk about His loving kindness and His desire to heal us.

I never have to feel alone. He is always with me. He answers prayers. He is faithful. And now I know with certainty, where I'm going after I leave this earth. I will be in the Kingdom of Heaven, basking in God's eternal love. I thank Him for all the blessings He has bestowed upon me. I hope and pray every human being on the earth will personally experience God's unending mercy and forgiveness. Everyone can be made whole again. It's really very simple. All you have to do is ask Him into your heart. May God richly bless you, one and all.

Prayer:

Today, dear Father in Heaven, we bring ourselves in the Presence of the Holy Spirit. We search for that mighty Great Spirit of Healing, that healing love which moves like the wind. It brings us the joy and the peace which accompanies Our Lord Jesus Christ. Dear Father in Heaven, we gather here in the power of Your Holy Spirit. We're asking for a mighty moving among each person here today, a moving with Your Presence of healing love. We ask that we might be faithful, we might be more obedient servants, that everything which is said today and done here today, sung and prayed will bring the honor and the glory to You, Father, Son, and Holy Spirit. Amen.

Let there be the gifts of the Holy Spirit, the gifts that St. Paul talks to us about in Galatians--peace and joy and tranquility. Let go of anything that is robbing you today, of the gift God wants for you today. Cleanse me, O Lord with Your holy blessing of purity and holiness and cleanliness. Take out of our hearts all coldness and bitterness; take out of our bodies all disease, whatever it might be that is stealing life from us, the gift you gave to us. Amen.

Helping Another Never to Give Up

You, my readers, through the acquiescence of this book have made a journey through its chapters; you have read three substantial sections:

Be a Winner, Not a Loser—Living in the Power of the Holy Spirit—True Stories from Weakness into Strength.

❖ What will you do with this motivational, psychological, and spiritual power? Give someone a break! This is the answer. Help another to look up to see the stars—not the mud.

❖ This is the mission of each human being—going into the arena of broken lives. This means to bring the message of God to the social gospel.

STORY TO REMEMBER:

When Lou Little was coaching football at Georgetown, he had a player who was definitely third rate but had so much spirit he was an inspiration to the team. He rarely saw action except in the last few minutes of a game that was already decided.

One day, news came that the boy's father had died. The youngster came to Little and said:

"Coach, I want to ask something of you that means an awful lot to me. I want to start the game against Fordham. I think that's what my father would have liked most." Little hesitated a moment, then said: "Okay, son, you'll start, but you'll only be in there for a play or two. You aren't quite good enough and you know it."

The boy started the game and played so well Little never took him out. His play inspired the team to victory. Back in the locker room Coach Little embraced the young man and said: "Son, you were terrific. You never played that way before…what got into you?"

The boy answered: "Remember how my father and I used to walk around arm-in-arm? There was something about him very few people knew—he was totally blind. This afternoon was the first time my father ever saw me play."

Therefore, my dear friends in Christ, you who have read these simple chapters, are being called to help another never to give up. In the famous words of the great Englishman and Statesman Sir Winston Churchill, may you be motivated to help another: **"Never give up. Never give up. Never give up." This was the commencement address, in its entirety, given to the British Naval Academy by Winston Churchill.**

SECTION VI

Only
A
Prayer Away

MOMENTS OF
PRAYER WHICH
TOUCH THE HEART
OF GOD

~QUIETNESS~

"Be still and know that I am God,"
That I who made and gave thee life
Will lead thy faltering steps aright;
That I who see each sparrow's fall
Will hear and heed thy earnest call.
I am God.

"Be still and know that I am God,"
When aching burdens crush thy heart,
Then know I form thee for thy part
And purpose in the plan I hold.
Trust in God.

"Be still and know that I am God,"
Who made the atom's tiny span
And set it moving to My plan,
That I who guide the stars above
Will guide and keep thee in My love.
Be thou still.

~Doran

THE POWER OF PRAYER HAS NO LIMITS

The Good Part:
"There is need of one thing only—Mary has chosen the good part...." (Luke 10: 42)

"No follower of Mine wanders in the dark; he shall have the light of life." (John 8: 12)

The Mystery of Miracles

by C. S. Lewis

"There is a sense in which no doctor ever heals...We speak for convenience of the doctor, or the dressing, healing the cut. But in another sense every cut heals itself: no cut can be healed in a corpse. That same mysterious force, which we call gravitational when it steers the planets and biochemical when it heals a live body, is the efficient cause of all recoveries. And that energy proceeds from God in the first instance. All who are cured are cured by Him, not merely in the sense that His Providence provides them with medical assistance and wholesome environments, but also in the sense that their very tissues are repaired by the far-descended energy which, flowing from Him, energizes the whole system of Nature. But once He did it visibly to the sick in Palestine, a Man meeting with men...The Power that always was behind all healings puts on face and hands."

A MORNING PRAYER

Sweet Jesus, lay Your wounded Hand upon my head and bless me. Stretch forth that same dear Hand and bless each one at home. And now give me Your Crook; I will return it to You tonight, and help me to go around in Your Fold, just for today, doing Your work in Your way.

Do not let the human in me spoil anything You give me to do. Push me back when I would go wrong and make me go forward when I am afraid to do right. Be with me in my dealings with each soul with whom I come in contact and grant each may know, love and serve You better for having passed me by.

One favor more. You will not think me presumptuous for You understand me. I want to know, love and serve You better than anyone else on earth and when life's little day is ended and its task complete give me a place at Your Feet to rest for all eternity.

Amen.

AT THE END OF THE DAY

Lord Jesus, we come to You for this evening
blessing, to seal within our hearts the inspirations
and the memories of this day. We ask You for Your
blessing and for the blessing of quietness for every
troubled heart, rest for every weary soul, and new
faith and courage for all who have faced exhausting
tasks this day. We would rest now in You. We are
tired, Lord. We would want to find in this evening
hour Your stillness and Your peace that bring us into
quiet harmony with Your Holy Will.

We give You thanks for every challenge that this
day has brought, every new vision of God that
winged its way across our skies, every whisper of
God that we sensed, every thought of God that
came in quiet moments, and every need of You that
brought us back to You in prayer. So now, dear
Father, grant us Your benediction. Watch over us
through the hours of darkness. Refresh us in Spirit
as well as in body as we sleep. Help us to face the
tasks of tomorrow, and may Your holy Presence and
Your guidance be always before us. Our Lord, bless
us.

Amen.

Prayer For Daily Devotions

A Soul in Union with God is Always in Springtime

The Apostles who loved and followed Jesus recognized an invisible Power dwelling within their Master and Lord Jesus.

"Domine, doce nos orare." "Lord, teach us to pray." Like the Apostles who daily lived and walked with Jesus so long ago, we too as they want to live in the Presence and the Power of God. All of us must storm the daily onslaughts which perilously endanger our journey to our heavenly home.

For this reason, we turn to our Master and Lord, Jesus, and we cravingly beseech Him: "Domine, doce nos orare—Lord, teach us to pray."

The following prayers—it is hoped—will serve you as stepping-stones for heart to speak to heart.

"Whatever you ask in My Name, I will do." (John 14: 13)

"At every opportunity pray in the Spirit, using prayers and petitions of every sort. Pray constantly and attentively for all in the holy company." (Ephesians 6: 18)

"Let the Word of Christ, rich as it is, dwell in you. In wisdom made perfect, instruct and admonish one another. Sing gratefully to God from your hearts in psalms, hymns and inspired songs." (Colossians 3: 16)

My dear Friends,

The following selection of prayers come to you as immediate props to activate the treasures of your spirit which are searching to be born into conversation with yourself, your Creator, and the world which awaits your intercessory prayer.

All of us—each and every one of us—need those silent moments to regain our earthly perspective. We all need to pray. In so doing it is necessary to find a private chamber for silent requiem and colloquy with heart that is human to heart that is divine. Will you, therefore, not seek the refreshing streams of living waters?

"For the lamb, which is in the midst of the thrones, shall rule them, and shall lead them to the fountains of the waters of life, and God shall wipe away all tears from their eyes."

ACT OF RECONCILIATION

Forgive me my sins, Lord Jesus, forgive me my sins; the sins of my youth, the sins of my age, the sins of my soul, the sins of my body, my idle sins, my serious voluntary sins, the sins I know, the sins I do not know; the sins I have concealed so long, and which are now hidden from my memory.

I am truly sorry for every sin, mortal and venial, for all the sins of my childhood up to this present hour.

I know my sins have wounded Thy tender heart, Jesus my Savior; let me be freed from the bonds of evil through Your most bitter passion.

Jesus, forget and forgive what I have been.

Come into my heart and be my personal Savior.

Amen.

IHS

A PRAYER FOR HEALING

Lord,
You invite all who are burdened to come to You.

Allow Your healing hand to heal me.

Touch my soul with Your compassion for others.

Touch my heart with Your courage and infinite love
for all.

Touch my mind with Your wisdom, that my mouth
may always proclaim Your praise.

Teach me to reach out to You in my need and help
me to lead others to You by my example.

Most loving Heart of Jesus, bring me health in
body, mind and spirit that I may serve You with all
my strength.

Touch gently this life which You have created, now
and forever.

I ask You, Jesus, to be the Lord of my life. Amen.

"Heal Us, O Lord, And Bring Us Together"

Father, You are the giver of all good things, the source of every blessing. You have called all people to be one in You and in each other. We pray that You will bless our healing ministry.

Send Your Holy Spirit to call Your people to this opportunity for spiritual renewal. Give us the insight, the courage, and the strength to truly change, that we may reflect the image of Your Son, Jesus.

May Your Healing Love penetrate our beings, prepare our hearts to receive You, and gift us with gratitude for Your abiding Presence. Grant us Lord Your Peace, Your Joy, and a fullness of Your Life for Your People.

𝔐𝔶 𝔏𝔬𝔯𝔡,
affirm me with the smile
of Your peace. Assure me
with the radiance of Your
Presence, O My Lord; as I
come before You, I see, as I
have never perceived
before, the "brokenness of
my person." I find it
difficult to talk to You. I
blush with embarrassment
over the state of my soul, the pointing finger of guilt, the
power of sin depersonalizing me, the consequences of sin
bursting like a wild unruly chain-explosion: they affect
me and my relationships. WHAT can I say, I who have
turned away from You so often with indifference? I have
been a stranger to prayer, undeserving of Your friendship
and Your love; I've been without honor and feel
unworthy. I am a weak and shallow creature, clever only
in the second-rate and worldly arts, seeking my comfort
and pleasure. Yes, I even gave my love—such as it was—
elsewhere. I put service to my earthly kings before my
duty to You. But now, my misfortune has brought me to
my knees, I have evaluated anew, I've come to my senses.
PLEASE, Lord, teach me how to serve You with all my
heart: to know at last what it really is to love, TO
ADORE. Help me, Lord, with the greatest gift You can
bestow upon me: TO BE ABLE TO DISCERN GOOD
AND EVIL. Help me, my Lord, that I may worthily
administer my Christian calling in accord with the
interests of "Your Kingdom" here upon earth, and find
my true honor in observing Your Divine Will. Please,
Lord, make me worthy.

THE HOUND OF
HEAVEN

I fled Him, down the nights and down the days;
I fled Him, down the arches of the years;
I fled Him down the labyrinthine ways
  Of my own mind; and in the midst of tears
I hid from Him, and under running laughter.
Up vistaed hopes I sped;
And shot, precipitated,
Adown titanic glooms of chasmed fears,
From those strong Feet that followed, followed
  after.
For, though I knew His love Who followed,
Yet was I sore adread
Lest having Him, I must have naught beside.
Still with unhurrying chase,
  And unperturbed pace,
Deliberate speed, majestic instancy,
  Came on the following feet,
  And a Voice above their beat—
Naught shelters thee, who wilt not shelter Me.

F. Thompson: The Hound of Heaven (19th cent.)

TO THE HOLY SPIRIT

O Holy Spirit, grant us health of mind and body and the fullness of Your grace. Sweet Holy Spirit, we ask You to descend upon each one of us, to fill us with Your gifts. We ask You to possess us, to baptize us in Your Spirit.

O Holy Spirit, we ask You to let us cherish the gift of love, the gift of life, the gift of joy, the gift of peace that comes from accepting You, the Divine Giver of all gifts. Oh give us the contentment that flows from being united with You! Use us to spread our religious experience, to spread the kingdom of praise to the world that needs to be burned with Your Divine Love. Help us, Holy Spirit, to be Your instruments of light to a dark world.
Amen.

Christ the King

Lord Jesus Christ, Son of the Living God, we hail You as our King! We recognize that through You, all things came to be; and in You will all things reach full growth. You are the image of Your Father, the richness of His grace, His free gift to us of life and love. From You, we have received the gift of Your own life to pulse within our spirits and make us truly sons and daughters of God our Father. With God's own love, You loved us, loved us to the end, and You shed Your Blood that we might live. With God's own love, You love us still, risen and in glory.

You share with us Your royal mission to bring the good news to the poor, to proclaim liberty to captives, and to set the downtrodden free.

Lord Jesus Christ, we hail You as our King and pledge to You our hearts and hands to help bring all mankind to Your holy throne and to bring Your boundless love, Your life, Your sacrifice, and the glorious freedom of the children of God to all men.

Sweet Son of the Living God, we welcome You to our hearts. Be the King of our souls! Remain with us, O Lord, and never depart. Amen.

SEVEN SPLENDID PSALMS

MOST PRECIOUS PRAYERS FOR SPIRITUAL RESTORATION

Jeremiah 30: 20
"For I will restore health to you and I will heal your wounds."

1. Psalm 6: "Lord, don't correct me when You are angry; Lord, have mercy on me because I am weak."
2. Psalm 31: "Lord, I trust in You. Listen to me and save me quickly."
3. Psalm 37: "Don't be upset because of evil people."
4. Psalm 50: "The God of gods, the Lord, speaks."
5. Psalm 101: "I will sing of Your love and fairness; Lord, I will sing praises to You. I will be careful to live an innocent life."
6. Psalm 129: "They have treated me badly all my life."
7. Psalm 142: "I cry out to the Lord; I pray to the Lord for mercy. I pour out my problems to Him; I tell Him my troubles."

SECTION VII

The Apostolate Of Divine Mercy And You....

"Mother of God's Son, Son of God's Mother"
~Dante

**The most beautiful scene in all the world:
A mother and her child**

Lovely Lady, Dressed in Blue
teach me how to pray!

God was just your little boy,
tell me what to say.

Did you lift Him up, sometimes,
gently on your knee?
Did you sing to Him the way Mother does to me?

Did you hold His hand at night?
Did you ever try telling Him stories of the world?
Oh! And did He cry?

Do you think He minds if I tell Him things–
just little things that happen?
And do the Angels' wings make a noise?

And can He hear me if I speak low?
Does He understand me now?
Tell me–for you know.

Lovely Lady, Dressed in Blue
teach me how to pray!

God was just your little boy,
and you know the way.

~Mary Dixon Thayer

THE APOSTOLATE OF DIVINE MERCY AND HEALING

IS NOTHING MORE THAN

AN APOSTOLATE OF PRAYER FOR HEALING / EVANGELISM

❖ The Apostolate of Divine Mercy and Healing is a Roman Catholic ecclesiastically approved mission of service to God's people. It administers primarily to Christians, both Catholic and Protestant, as well as non-Christians and the unchurched. The Apostolate bears within its essence an ecclesiastical recognition, discernment, and authorization of a valid charism of holistic healing. Its ultimate role—the salvation of man, is served by the efficient cause of Christian Evangelization utilizing its primary visible ministry of healing. cf. St. Thomas: Invisibilia per visibilia *(The invisible through the visible.)*

❖ The motto of the Apostolate of Divine Mercy and Healing is centered upon the principle: SANATIO HOMINIS....PROPAGANDA FIDEI; namely, the healing of man in its visible form rendering itself solely as an occasion to create faith in the Person of Jesus Christ and in His Divine Salvation Message. The Apostolate utilizes as its dynamics the proclamation of the Gospel to the people of today. It is a service rendered to the Christian community and to the whole of humanity. The Gospel is proclaimed as "Good News." It proclaims two fundamental commands:

"PUT ON THE NEW SELF" (Ephesians 4: 24)
"BE RECONCILED TO GOD" (2 Cor. 5: 20)

❖ The Apostolate of Divine Mercy and Healing has its
authoritative functioning, for both the local church of
its origin, Worcester Diocese, and for its outreach
mission outside of Worcester, directly from its Roman
Catholic Ordinary, formerly Bishop Bernard J.
Flanagan, D.D. and Bishop Timothy J. Harrington,
D.D., and presently Bishop Daniel P. Reilly, D.D., the
residing Ordinary of Worcester, Mass. Such an
Apostolate, with its essence and nature, having been
experientially proven by time and with constancy, as
well as its good effects for the benefit of God's people
and the upholding of the Church's doctrine, is at the
disposal of the Roman Catholic bishops both within
the United States and abroad, if so desired.

❖ The Apostolate of Divine Mercy and Healing seeks
Divine Healing and **Divine Restoration** of man's
holistic person. First, man's spiritual relationship to
his God by an increase and a development of the
theological virtues of faith, hope, and love. Secondly, it
seeks man's psychological growth, both to his own
personal value and self-acceptance, and to his
emotional interpersonal relationships to society.
Thirdly, it directs itself to physical restoration from
diseases or accidents. Through such a ministry, one
who is chosen distinctively, functions in the
personification of the gift's author, Jesus Christ.
Thereupon he/she becomes a vessel or a conduit of
God's actual grace. In consequence of that, healing and
restoration flow into the lives of God's people.

❖ The Apostolate's goal is "The Salvation of Man" through God's healing power. It has three objectives:

WHOLENESS—EXCELLENCE—OUTREACH

WHOLENESS is the foundation for everything one does. It is training in harmony, training holistically. It is wholeness in mind so as to learn about God and about people. It refers to being fit. It refers to having a sound mind and a sound body. It helps one to worship, praise, and love God.

EXCELLENCE signifies superiority as in self-worth. The Apostolate helps people to give God their best, and to expect from God His best. This is based upon the truth that God Does Love You!

OUTREACH is to reach beyond one's own reach. Herein, it signifies bringing God's power to all people. It seeks to give God's power away. To give God's power away means to do something with our lives. We thus bring God's power through our lives to everyone; we go into all ways of life and living. We practically help people to look directly to God as their source—nobody else, nothing else! God alone is the source of our life; and He sustains it because God really is concerned about His people. God wants the best for His people. Being so disposed, we go forth in Jesus' name: we touch, we love, we suffer with the people. We bring hope through healing. We are not afraid to boldly launch out into deeper waters.

❖ The Apostolate presents itself to the public solely in the general functioning of the Church as Missionary in Evangelization and the charismatic affirmation of the Gospel through healing signs and wonders. It offers a service of mission for the whole purpose of the Church; namely, to teach and evangelize the Person of Jesus Christ and His Gospel. The theme of Evangelization has always been the tool of the Church. With this tool, the Church for all the ages of its existence has, is and will continue to engender in its hearers FAITH IN THE PERSON OF JESUS CHRIST. It is only in the Christian message that modern man will find the answer to his questions as well as energy for his commitment to human solidarity.

❖ In the personality of this specific Apostolate, a validly discerned charism of healing (gifts of healing) is utilized. It expresses itself as a visible conduit or a stepping-stone to initially impart the gift of faith in the non-believer or the unchurched (Propagatio Fidei /conversion effect). Moreover, it influences the Christian people, both Catholics and Protestants, into a fuller appreciation of the faith in Jesus Christ and His Gospel already dwelling within them through the valid baptism of water. This is the "Propaganda Fidei" effect / the proclaiming of the faith. It is to this functioning duty that the Apostolate of Divine Mercy and Healing identifies itself and perceives its mighty dynamics.

The kernel and center of Christ's Good News is salvation. It is God's gift of liberation from everything that oppresses mankind. Above all, it is a liberation from sin and the evil one.

The Gospel has the power of hidden energy. It has the power to heal the total person. Above all, it has the influence to effect man's conscience. It transforms lives. Christ proclaims the Gospel of God through preaching, teaching and by signs and wonders which confirm the spoken Gospel. Those who accept this Gospel will have been gathered into the Christian community of salvation. They, in turn, are impelled by some inner spiritual command to boldly communicate and to share it with others. This is Christian witnessing. This is the concept of soulwinning. Like the Apostles of the primitive church, their voice has gone out to the limits of the earth, their words to the end of the world. They proclaimed what God has done for them, and they grasp the meaning of His Deeds.

❖ The Apostolate realistically recognizes itself as a universal tool for teaching and preaching. The Church exists in order to Evangelize! It preaches, it teaches, it becomes a channel of grace to heal.

The Apostolate, moreover, observes itself from its effects as a link of unity between the primitive Christian Church and the present contemporary expression of Church. This principle belief and practice has been the powerful force by which bishops from other dioceses have evaluated, accepted, and utilized this ministry. It is our hope that this Divine Mission Call will continue to be used to evangelize God's people through Christ in the unity of the Holy Spirit. May God continue to give birth to all our strengths. May God instill in all of us the boldness of the Apostles who fearlessly went forth and launched out into deeper waters with God as their only source.

THANK YOU

Dear Friends,

You have made the journey through this book accompanied by its various reflections. It is my sincerest hope that the moments of reading have led your spirit into a deeper love of the God above who likes you and loves you.

I personally promise you as I have done over the past forty-seven years since the day of my Ordination, June 1, 1957, that each day when I am privileged to raise up the holy bread of Eucharist and in the raising up on high my silver and golden chalice designed in the image of Our Lady of Lourdes, Mother of the Sick, you and all your loved ones will have a special spot of remembrance where remembrances are the most preciously held.

I bless you, in gratitude, for your time and your journey with me through this book.

May the blessing of Almighty God the Father, the Son, and the Holy Spirit be upon you; and may the protection of the Holy Mother of God be always with you until the end of time and your entrance into the agelessness of eternity wherein you will experience God's Embracing Love.

MOTHER OF THE DIVINE PROVIDENCE

"O Holy Virgin, in the midst of your glorious days do not forget the sadness of the world. Turn a look of kindness upon those who are in suffering, who are in the midst of difficulties, and who cease not to struggle against the misfortunes of this life. Have pity on those who love and are separated. Have pity on the loneliness of the heart. Have pity on the feebleness of my own faith and the faith of others who remain feeble in their brokenness, despair and emptiness. Have pity! Have pity on the objects of our tenderness, my tenderness. Have pity on all those who weep, on all those who pray, on all those who fear. Give each one of us—give me, give us, the hope of peace. We ask this through the birth, death, resurrection and ascension of Christ. Amen."